BIG IMPACT GIVING

MIKE SKRYPNEK

What others are saying about Mike Skrypnek:

———————

"*Mike and I have volunteered together on the Gift Planning Advisory Committee of the Canadian Cancer Society. Mike has a giving heart and I would consider him a subject matter expert in the area of strategic and planned giving.*"

– DARCY HULSTON, CEO Canoe Financial

———————

Big praise for BIG IMPACT GIVING

———————

"*Mike is a results based high integrity professional who always has his clients' interests foremost. He is engaging, thoughtful and fearless. In my over 30 years management experience Mike would rate in the top three best consultants I have ever worked with. His book, Big Impact Giving, is a quick and easily understood guide that Canadian baby boomers can put to work today in their legacy planning.*"

– DAN HOLINDA, CEO Canadian Cancer Society, AB/NWT

"We all will be remembered for one of two things. The problems we created when we were alive, or the ones we solved. If you wish to be in the latter group Mike's Big Impact Giving will show you how. Consider this book you now hold in your hands a step-by-step guide that provides a clear path for truly making a positive difference ... both now and in the future!"

— KEITH THOMSON, Canadian Director of the *Donor Motivation Program*™

"Big Impact Giving, *simply and clearly combines the why and the how of philanthropy. Mike is able to convey the deeply personal meaning of legacy through his wonderful stories, while giving the reader a clear path to implementing their own strategic legacy giving. I would recommend this book to anyone who is serious about making a big impact through their charitable giving.*"

— MARILYN SUEY, Principal of Yerba Buena Wealth Advisors, LLC. Author, speaker and business consultant.

About Mike

Mike is an accomplished author and speaker. He is recognized as Canada's leading authority on strategic legacy giving and is an expert at guiding families to realize a bigger impact in their lives and beyond. He has  delivered motivating presentations for entrepreneurs, lawyers, financial planners, charities and their donors. Speaking to audiences of 20 to 200 people, Mike has entertained and inspired over 1,600 people in just the past two years. Through his guidance, he has helped re-direct over $2.4 million to charitable causes while helping save over $1.1 million in current income and estate taxes, since 2012, and he has a lot more to do.

Mike's BIG IMPACT GIVING process makes estate and legacy planning purposeful. He has been a member of the Professional Advisor's Committee of the Calgary Foundation, member of the roundtable for the Canadian Association of Gift Planners – Southern Alberta and member of the Canadian Cancer Society (AB/NWT) Gift Planning Advisory Cabinet. He also is an advisor to numerous non-profit organizations throughout Calgary.

Mike and his family have been actively involved in volunteering and fundraising in Calgary for the past 25 years. Their family charitable fund is the "Fit Family Fund".

He knows life without passion and purpose is a life wasted and he is dedicated to showing others how they can achieve their BIG IMPACT GIVING.

Help others achieve their Big Impact Giving!

Share this book!

Retail: $14.95

Special Quantity Discounts

5 — 20 books	$13.95
21 — 50 books	$12.95
100 — 499 books	$10.95
500 + books	$9.95

To place an order, contact:

(403) 870-6775

info@BigImpactGiving.ca

www.BigImpactGiving.ca

"Buy the book"

CONTENTS

About Mike   v

Bonus   vi

Foreword   ix

Author's Note   xi

INTRODUCTION
1

PHILANTHROPY
THE BASICS

8

STAGE 1
17

STAGE 2
26

STAGE 3
47

STAGE 4
63

STAGE 5
86

Acknowledgments   96

FOREWORD

If you are a "baby boomer", born in the period from 1946 through 1964, you are part of a generation that has shaped the world we live in like no other generation in history. You have influenced our buying, health, planning, housing, clothing and eating habits. You have also shaped the way we invest and save money. Between your home, your recreational property and your registered and non-registered savings plans, and pensions, you have amassed enough wealth to retire with and support you the rest of your life. You may be the "millionaire next door". Now you stand at a planning precipice. There is a window of time, which you are in today, where you are considering a transition from working to either partial or full retirement. As you determine whether you'll have enough to live on, and if you are convinced you do, you will also be thinking about your heirs and the community at large. There are perils that exist when you contemplate passing on your wealth, such as taxes; but *Big Impact Giving* gives you the education and tools to help you combine sensible financial legacy planning with charitable giving to make a significant impact in this world, while protecting and preserving your assets and legacy for the benefit of your heirs.

In this book, Mike Skrypnek's second on the topic of philanthropy, you are provided a guide to giving that incorporates what it means to be philanthropic, and the common stages of that journey. Each step of the way, Mike has provided very helpful insight, tips and guides to help you implement giving through your own personal journey of philanthropy.

As the founder of Canada's leading independent Donor Advised Fund provider, BenefAction Foundation, I have the pleasure of meeting and working with the nation's most philanthropically minded advisors. There are few that have the combined knowledge and philanthropic passion that Mike does. There are even fewer who are so willing and prominent in sharing that information with people, like you, who can benefit from it the most.

Enjoy this quick read, a simple and pointed guide to BIG IMPACT GIVING.

Nicola Elkins,
CEO & Founder of BenefAction

AUTHOR'S NOTE

This book was written specifically for North America's baby boomers — you know who you are, but if you don't that's the lot of you born between 1946 and 1964. You are between 50 and 68 years old this year. Your generation has the resources required to change the face of philanthropy and have the most significant impact ever on giving.

Right now, you control or influence nearly 75% of North America's invested assets. On average, in the next 10 to 15 years, you will begin planning for the transfer of the largest amount of wealth to the next generation in the history of the world.

Most of you are approaching and planning for retirement. Some of you recognize your true net worth, but not everyone understands that as homeowners, often with recreational and/or income properties, as well as registered retirement plans and non-registered long-term appreciated assets, you are probably worth over $1 million. That does make you the "millionaire next door"!

What can you do to preserve and protect the value of your estate and ensure a successful transfer of wealth in the face of multiple threats, the most significant being taxes?

I help baby boomers, whether they're individuals or families, address their concerns and look to the future.

Fortunately, you can plan for and minimize taxes. Because our government recognizes that generally speaking charities are better than government when it comes to addressing some of our biggest social challenges, the government incentivizes taxpayers to re-direct their tax dollars to charity.

I'm here to tell you that charitable giving is the best way to re-direct your tax dollars while planning the transfer of your estate. Insurance is another highly effective tool that is rarely used as well as it could be to minimize your tax burden.

Together, charitable giving and insurance can significantly reduce the taxes you'll pay while maximizing the value of your estate and giving back to the causes, communities and organizations that truly matter to you.

Get ready to learn more about how you can realistically and legitimately plan for a zero-tax estate while giving back to make a difference!

INTRODUCTION

——————•——————

phi·lan·thro·py

*The desire to promote the welfare of others,
expressed especially by the generous donation
of money to good causes*

— Oxford Dictionaries

As a boomer, you want to plan for a zero-tax estate but many of you also want to make sure your giving has a BIG IMPACT — I want to share what I've learned about how you can do that.

Baby boomers in North America control over 80% of the individual financial assets and over half of the consumer spending. Two thirds of Boomers want to pass their inheritance to their family while the rest are looking to direct theirs to charities.

But, unless you properly prepare and plan, a good chunk of your hard-earned cash will definitely go to the government where it will not have the big impact it would if you had strategically set up your charitable giving.

I don't have anything against the government but I care deeply about how that money could be better used to help the people that truly need it. Over the years, I've seen the effects of random, spontaneous acts of giving that were inspired by an individual's involvement with a particular individual or cause. I've also seen the results when people consistently practice committed philanthropy over the long term.

In fact, when I was in my 20s, I was a prime example of

"involved giving" as the owner of a personal training and athletic therapy agency. Back then, in-line skating was a new activity — a bit of a fad — and it seemed everyone was either on Rollerblades™ or talking about them. To give back to charity and raise our agency's profile, I organized *Get In-line with Cystic Fibrosis*" — an old fashioned skate-a-thon.

Why did I decide to raise money for Cystic Fibrosis?

When giving, most of us are motivated by some sort of personal connection and so was I.

Back in high school, laughing, smiling Danielle was a dear friend of mine, who typically missed a week of school every single month to have the phlegm sucked out of her lungs at a local children's hospital. Born with cystic fibrosis, that treatment kept Danielle from drowning from the inside out. Not many of our schoolmates knew why she was absent so much.

We were teens and we felt invincible and it simply didn't occur to us that Danielle might not make it to adulthood.

While in university, I made friends with Jody, another young woman with cystic fibrosis. We were acquaintances for two years until she died — at 21 years of age!

A couple of years later, although Danielle and I had lost touch, I heard that Danielle was on the waiting list for a lung transplant.

I couldn't help Jody! I needed to do something for Danielle and everyone like her.

"Get in Line with Cystic Fibrosis", my first ever charity event, raised a few thousand dollars and I felt better.

What motivates us to open up our hearts and wallets or volunteer our time? Studies have shown the number one reason that we give is that we have a feeling of compassion for those in need. A personal connection to a cause and/or being personally affected by a specific issue, and a desire to give back to the community will also drive us to act. For most people, the potential tax and financial implications rank below all of those when it comes to charitable motivations.

In fact, according to the Statistics Canada Survey of Giving, Volunteering and Participating, conducted in 2004 and 2007, less than one out of four of respondents stated that the related tax benefits were the driving force behind their philanthropy. In my role as a professional philanthropic advisor, I've seen that the expected effects on taxable income do play a significant role in the *size* of the gift or legacy but *not* in the commitment to giving.

We all live unique lives and have a broad range of experiences with a wide variety of people to which each of us reacts differently. Who has affected how you think? Which experience has had a lasting effect on how you behave?

For every single one of us, the desire to give back started somewhere — where was that for you?

I'm here to help you explore philanthropy and identify the practical and effective steps you can take to have a big impact on the people, causes, and organizations you care about.

All giving is good, yet certain types of giving are much more effective and impactful than others. We give to share, we give to help and we give to feel good. It gives us purpose and leading a purposeful life is fundamentally important to humanity.

I categorize giving in two ways. There are distinct kinds of giving: *involved giving* and *committed philanthropy*.

What's the difference?

Involved giving connects us with someone or something that we are concerned with and care about. It's often emotional and personal — that's why we typically react and act spontaneously and impulsively.

The result?

To help right now, we might give cash, buy an item at an auction or a bake sale, or donate to disaster victims. We might volunteer or even sponsor someone or something without much thought. Whatever we do, it feels right and we feel better for having done it.

Looking back, I can see that my "Get in Line with Cystic Fibrosis" event was something I'd now consider *involved* giving rather than *committed* philanthropy. As much as I wanted to make life better for people like Danielle and Jody, the impact was definitely one-time and short-term.

On the other hand, what I call *committed* philanthropy is a way of life that is focused on giving back in ways that maximize the impact. It is methodical, planned, and always present because these committed philanthropists are intent on taking actions that make the world a better place *every* day.

As the millionaire next door, you can be as committed and effective a philanthropist as Bill and Melinda Gates, Oprah, or Richard Branson. Of course, their various resources are well beyond what most of us can even imagine, yet we can and do share the desire to have a long-term, big impact. Like them, we can do the research and strategic planning that is the foundation of committed philanthropy. We can identify, implement, and sustain the actions required to deliver big results month to month long after we're gone.

Today, I'm completely focused on *committed* philanthropy, professionally and personally. Every day, I look at how I can use my strengths, knowledge and experience to help others find their philanthropic path and maximize their impact on their charity of choice.

In late 2008, I established my family's Fit Family Fund, which focuses on family health and nutrition, education, protection of children, and youth sports, all of which are incredibly important to us.

The Fit Family Fund is important to me because it helps me support the kind of kids I grew up with in a small transient community in Calgary, along the Bow River. As a little kid, I could see that they were often sick, unbathed, or wore the same clothes over and over again. As an adult, I was able to recognize the patterns of poverty, abuse, addiction, and dysfunctional family life. I came to understand that where they ended up in life had nothing to do with being lazy, unintelligent, or plain bad.

Back then, I didn't recognize that they needed help, I didn't know how to help, and I didn't have the necessary resources.

I was very fortunate growing up. I have loving parents and had a great childhood with a lot of opportunity. As a result, I'm now an adult with the ability to help the kids who need our Fit Family Fund today.

Committed philanthropy is a shift from feeling connected to being immersed and I'm looking forward to sharing what I've learned through my experiences as a philanthropic speaker, donor, and advisor and through my observations of others' giving experiences.

Every single week, I meet donors who regularly give relatively small amounts, but when I show them how they can position their finances and assets to reduce or eliminate taxes, thus realizing much larger legacy gifts, they are motivated to become even more committed to philanthropy.

When people ponder their wealth/assets, they are far more concerned with their families, friends, and causes, than their bank rolls. People have a natural desire to give back and while the motivation is typically highly personal, the tools are often financial.

How does one person make an impact without the public profile, connections, or resources of Oprah or the Gates'? As individuals, we might not make a significant dent, but as a collective, we will have a significant cumulative effect that will have a massive impact.

Canadians like to think of themselves as compassionate, socially-minded, and generous, but when it comes to tangible financial gifts, Canadians give less than one percent (0.8) of our income — half of what the average American donates.

Even when each Canadian's average charitable donation is less than one percent, that's still $10 billion annually. Imagine what Canada's 86,000 registered charities could do with double the money.

Why don't donors give more? They may be overwhelmed by the sheer number of charities that support the causes that resonate with them. They might find it daunting, even intimidating to research and identify the charities that will make the best use of their money. In addition to the existing, 86,000 charities in 2012, 1,932 of those were brand new and 3,900 had also applied for their charitable registration.

They might also be legitimately concerned by the fact more than 1,600 charities lose or relinquish their charitable status in Canada in a typical year. Will their money really be used to help the targeted people/cause? Will it be used for administration and marketing costs? Could their money be wasted or stolen?

Obviously, I'm passionate about committed philanthropy, but why should you trust me to help you figure which charities should get how much of your money?

I hold a variety of investment management credentials and I'm an Accredited Investment Fiduciary Professional (AIFP®) and a Fellow of the Canadian Securities Institute which has been particularly valuable when working with endowments and foundations.

In the past few years, I've shared my BIG IMPACT GIVING™ process with 1,605 donors, investors, lawyers, accountants, financial advisors and philanthropic professionals in Canada and the United States and I look forward to continuing these conversations to help inspire more committed philanthropy.

In previous roles as a member of the Professional Advisor's Committee of The Calgary Foundation, the Canadian Association of Gift Planners — Southern Alberta Roundtable and the Gift Planning Advisory Cabinet for the Canadian Cancer Society, I have provided advice, guidance, and direction to a range of charities, businesses and individuals.

Since late 2012, I have helped a number of families direct $2,443,337 to charitable causes and saved them more than $1,118,000 in current income and future estate taxes.

My goal?

I want to lead and guide you through a series of steps that will set you on the path to truly committed philanthropy in a manner that ensures sustainability.

I'll help you get total clarity on why you want to give back and who you want to help. We'll look at which financial tools will have the big impact on your charity of choice while delivering the maximum benefits to your estate over the long term.

In short, I'll help you learn how to:

- connect to your cause
- pick the charity that reflects your values and goals
- deliver the big impact to the charity of your choice and your estate
- give more while leaving more
- show gratitude for what you have and what you've achieved

Let's get started!

PHILANTHROPY

the basics

•———————•

As defined by your dictionary of choice, philanthropy can seem a little impersonal, even sterile. According to Merriam-Webster, philanthropy is the practice of giving money and time to help make life better for other people, but that dictionary definition doesn't even touch on the connections made, the emotions experienced, the lives changed, or the personal journeys that bring people to the moment of giving.

Not too long ago, I met John for coffee at a ridiculously small table in a crowded café, where we chatted about what had happened when he donated money to a charity recommended by his friend Steve during a game of golf. Equally inspired by both Steve's commitment and the charity's need, John met with his financial advisor who recommended he sell some stock, then donate some of the proceeds. His advisor pointed out that the charitable contribution tax credit would help offset the capital gains taxes he had to pay on the stock he'd sold.

After selling his stock to make that donation, John learned that the charity actually used his money to pay its rent — the month before it was evicted! In hindsight it was all too easy to see that he should have done his homework on the organization before he made the donation.

What could John have done differently to preserve his capital and ensure his hard-earned funds didn't go to waste?

As a philanthropic consultant and financial advisor, I want every donor to know how to best leverage their available funds while minimizing or eliminating the taxes. By directly donating the shares *instead* of selling them, he wouldn't have had to pay *any* capital gains tax *and* as an added bonus, he could have given more to the charity. Quite simply, his financial advisor either didn't know the best strategy or was protecting his own interests, through triggering a transaction, before his client's.

Going forward, my friend now knows that before he gives to any charity, he'll use resources such as the Canada Revenue Agency charity information website to do a background check that will reveal basic, but vital financial information. I also recommend running organizations that interest you through local and community foundations, www.Place2Give.com, www.Goodworks.ca, and www.imaginecanada.ca.

As the café emptied, we talked more about what John can do to maximize the value and impact of his next gift and ensure he and the beneficiaries reap the maximum benefits.

Fortunately, some givers have infinitely better giving experiences from the outset, for example, Jim and Anne (not their real names) who I met at one of my tax and estate planning presentations. In their late 60s, they were both retired and living comfortably on their pensions, while giving about $1,500 in cash to a handful of charities that were important to them each year.

However, Jim and Anne were concerned when they learned their registered retirement plans would be heavily taxed when it came time to settle their estate. They were truly horrified by the realization that once they were gone, their cottage would be subject to such considerable capital gains tax their children might be forced to sell it to pay the bill.

They asked me to help them protect their wealth against threats such as taxation, ensure they could consistently give more to charity and preserve their legacy, while leaving as much as possible for their children.

About ten months later, with my guidance, Jim and Anne

had embraced a more methodical, strategic, and planned approach to long-term giving that will donate far more to charity, protect their estate for their children and eliminate up to $250,000 in taxes due when their estate is settled.

First and foremost, they set up a donor-advised fund — a charitable-giving vehicle created specifically to manage charitable donations on behalf of an organization, family, or individual. When Jim and Anne pass on, the children or another named individual or organization, for example, an accountant or lawyer, would then direct the funds to one or more charities.

A donor-advised fund is an effective tax and estate planning tool, since each year that the donor contributes to the donor-advised tax fund, they receive a tax credit/deduction.

In Jim and Anne's case, the creation of the donor-advised fund and their initial contribution provided an immediate fifty per cent tax credit and going forward, they will reap that reward at that moment, every year that they put money into the fund.

I've found that the men and women who set up donor-advised funds also use them to help share and transfer their social awareness and philanthropic values to their young, or adult, children and others who matter to them.

I also suggested Jim and Anne invest in a new life insurance policy that was tailored to their unique needs and circumstances. While Jim and Anne had assumed a new life insurance policy was impossible because they're in their late 60s, they did fortunately qualify for life insurance. Rather than make an assumption, always do the research, ask the right questions and get the facts.

What's the final impact?

Jim, Anne, and I had determined that the likely future tax due on the remaining spouse's RRIF and the capital gains tax on the cottage would total roughly $250,000. The $500,000 donation to charity, which was made possible by the new insurance policy and the new donor-advised fund, would create a $250,000 tax credit that completely offset the taxes owed. Because there are no other taxable concerns, we were able to structure things in such a way that the children will inherit their parents' entire estate tax-free.

As a result of the Big Impact Giving process that Anne and Jim worked through with me, they are able to leave an amazing legacy gift of $500,000 and still support the charities that had relied on their $1,500 a year.

Jim and Anne are thrilled that they will leave the causes and charities that matter to them with a gift that's far beyond what they ever imagined was within their reach, while allowing their children to keep the much-loved family cottage with all of its traditions and memories.

As importantly, Jim and Anne now have the insights and guidelines required to identify and then thoroughly investigate the charities that resonate with them because they reflect their own relationships and experiences. Jim and Anne are also paying close attention to which charities will most effectively use their gift(s) to help the intended people and causes as well as which charities really need the help.

Another couple, Barbara and Graham, already supported several charities and were in the throes of developing a detailed, long-range giving plan and investigating multiple organizations. However, in late November, the pair also faced an immediate challenge in the form of Graham's substantial retirement package which was sure to result in a hefty, nearly six-figure tax bill. On my recommendation, they established a donor-advised fund for their family to which he made a six-figure contribution just before Christmas. As a result, the six-figure amount was redirected from Revenue Canada to the fund and gave them time to properly investigate how they would give in the future to a charity of their choice.

At this point, I expect you're getting a much better understanding of the difference between a spontaneous, emotionally-driven gift and a strategically-planned gift in terms of both process and the ultimate results. The impulsive donation, whether it's $1, $10 or even $1,000 is an involved gift that typically helps the donor feel good right now.

We all like things that give us an immediate and palpable sense of pleasure and scientific studies have shown giving tends to make the benefactor or giver happier than the beneficiary, although we'd expect the reverse to be true.

Planned giving requires more time and effort because it demands committed research and attention to detail. On top of that, planned giving invariably produces the biggest impact *after* we die. Now that you know that, you know exactly why random giving is so much more appealing.

However, I do recognize and accept that involved, random, or spontaneous giving does have its place and can effectively deliver the required results. For example, the Salvation Army's Christmas Kettle Campaign, which has been around for more than 120 years and has over 2,000 locations Canada-wide, depends heavily on the nickels, dimes, quarters, loonies and twoonies that virtually every passerby will contribute. Altogether, each of these small contributions will help the Salvation Army help 1.6 million people who need food, clothing, and shelter.

Random or involved giving to credible, legitimate not-for-profits like the Salvation Army ensures your money serves the intended purpose. However, a spontaneous gift to an organization that you didn't properly vet isn't any better than not giving. If the organization is poorly run or a scam, your gift might be wasted or stolen, which renders your donation virtually worthless despite your good intentions.

There is always a time, a place, and an occasion for one-off giving, but I'd still like you to stop and think before you give your money away. Why? While every gift means something to both the donor and beneficiary, you now recognize that intent and impact are often vastly different.

Spontaneous, random, involved giving is fun and it feels good. Better yet, it takes less time, effort, and thought than committed philanthropy. However, it rarely has the impact on either the benefactor or the beneficiaries as the same amount of money would if you'd put more time, effort, and thought into the planning and research.

When you know that you want your gifts to have more impact, regardless of the monetary amount or the level of volunteerism, you have a moral responsibility to ensure your philanthropy is being used in the most effective way possible to maximize the results.

When you just want to get to the feel-good giving, the investigating, assessing your charity, then analyzing potential results and outcomes can seem impersonal, even painstakingly tedious. Yet, the very fact that it is your money means it is always highly personal! Taking a carefully considered, business-like approach to how *your* money will be used and how it will help you, your estate, and the charity is quite simply the smart thing to do.

You worked smart and hard to make that money. Doesn't the vast amount of time and effort you put into making that money warrant the same degree of commitment around deciding which charity really needs, deserves, or has earned the fruits of your decades-plus labours?

Absolutely!

Does that mean the process I'm suggesting you build into your approach to committed philanthropy has to be either complex or tiresome?

Absolutely not!

Do I want you to analyse, research, plan, and strategize every donation and every good deed?

Yes!

As a philanthropic advisor, I know that every donor, from the millionaire boomers next door to philanthropic icons such as Oprah, Richard Branson, and the Gates', travelled through five key stages on their philanthropic journeys, whether or not they recognized them as such.

In the following chapters, I will provide a how-to-guide that will lead you through stages 1 to 5:

- ⟫ STAGE ONE: How do you connect to philanthropy? What matters to you?

- ⟫ STAGE TWO: What cause resonates with you and which charity will you support?

- ⟫ STAGE THREE: What are your unique resources, capabilities, or strengths?

- ⟫ STAGE FOUR: What will you do? How? When?

- ⟫ STAGE FIVE: What are you thankful for? What did you learn?

The process around committed philanthropy is much like the process you'd follow around any significant commitment, such as the purchase of a vehicle.

First and foremost, you'd think about who you are and what you want. Will this vehicle reflect your personality and what matters to you while also suiting your lifestyle?

Once you've determined what you want and need, you'd do the research to identify and locate the vehicle(s) that meet your unique needs and goals. You'd likely leverage the power of the Internet as well as the available experts and of course, your peers to access a wealth of data and viewpoints. You'd acknowledge, that like it or not, certain brands and their public images have already made an impression.

So, you'd do what it takes to assess the vehicle(s) as objectively and as closely as possible, which could include one or even several test drives. You'd carefully compare the various features, options and costs, then review the financing. You might take a few days or even weeks to further weigh your decision.

You would probably do this for more than one vehicle because you want to be sure it's the right one even though it's a depreciable asset that won't earn you the tax benefits you'll realize with charitable donations.

Shouldn't you be willing to invest at least as much brain power, time, and effort in the charity you support as you would in the process you'd apply to buying a vehicle — an expense that delivers no tangible financial benefits whatsoever!

Your life experiences
connect you to your
philanthropic purpose

*"Experience is not what happens to a man; it is
what a man does with what happens to him."*

— Aldous Huxley, *Texts & Pretexts:
An Anthology with Commentaries*

———◦———

We all have life experiences and it's often our reactions to
those experiences that shape the individuals we become. Some
experiences barely leave a mark, while others will remain
deeply engraved on our psyches and will affect our world view
forever, whether or not we're aware of it.

Our individual life experiences invariably affect how we
connect to other people and it's these connections that inspire
us to act for others.

When looking at our life experiences from a philanthropic
vantage point, we are really looking at everything that will
lead us to the causes that matter so much to us we'll choose to
support, fund, and improve them.

As you may remember, my high-school and college
era friendships with Danielle and Jody, both of whom
were profoundly affected by cystic fibrosis, motivated my
old-fashioned "Get In-line with Cystic Fibrosis" skate-a-thon
when I was in my twenties. Decades later, the memory of
the kids I grew up with, kids who are now adults and whom
I haven't seen in more than 35 years, prompted the launch of
my own family's Fit Family Fund in 2008 with its focus on
keeping children safe, getting them healthy, and giving them
an education.

Like me, your desire to help others might have started when
you realized just how fortunate you were to grow up the way

you did. Conversely, if you struggled through childhood to succeed as an adult, your hardship may be what inspires you to help the ones that are living the childhood or teenage years that you did.

While our life experiences and philanthropic commitments will be as individual as we are, our respective experiences always form the foundations on which our ideas about giving are built.

To define the experiences that shaped us, there are questions we need to ask ourselves. What events, circumstances, or relationships shaped your ideas about how the world gives to people or takes from them? Were you hungry? Did you have access and funding for your education that your peers did not? Did you benefit from incredible opportunities that few people will ever experience? Were you physically or emotionally threatened? Did you live in fear for your safety or your family's?

How did you react to these experiences? How did you change as a result?

Over the past three decades, I have studied modern philanthropic icons and have been privileged to work with and interview some great philanthropists as well as the men and women who lead bottom-line oriented businesses and not-for-profit organizations. I have learned that regardless of the roles these people hold today, they were all connected to their philanthropic passions by one or more of these six human experiences. Whether the person experienced the positive or the negative personally or vicariously, it has an impact that moves them to reach out and help out.

SIX CRITICAL HUMAN EXPERIENCES:

FAMILY: Did the family unit provide unconditional love and support to the individual as a newborn, toddler, child, teen, and young adult? Was there physical, sexual, or mental/emotional abuse?

SCARCITY, POVERTY, SUBSISTENCE: Access to sufficient nutritious food and clean water as well as housing, clothing, and medical and dental care should be a given — it's not.

AFFLUENCE: Earned or inherited, the affluent often reach out because they recognize such wealth is a rarity.

EDUCATION: The ability to read and write at a certain level and access to an education should be a given — again — it's not.

PHYSICAL AND MENTAL CHALLENGES, ILLNESS, AND DISEASE: Debilitating injury or illness and physical or mental health challenges have a lifelong impact on the individual and the people close to them. They affect everything from their mental, emotional, and physical well-being to their finances and earning ability.

SAFETY AND SECURITY: Did a military regime, political doctrine, religious belief, or even gender inequity pose a physical, mental, or emotional threat?

To identify what is important to you, you have to look at how life has affected you.

Think about your life, then get a pen and work through the following questions.

Remember, these are big, open-ended questions that ask you to sift through a lifetime's worth of experiences — the good and the bad, the joyful and the agonizing.

Rummaging around in the memory banks will demand

time and energy. Reminiscing can be fun. It can also be painful. Just know that ultimately it will reward you by helping uncover your true path to philanthropy.

If you can't get started or reach an impasse, go back and take another look at the six critical human experiences that we know tie us to charity. Which ones resonate with you? Why? Feel free to make a few notes, and then tackle the questions again.

Fill in the blanks, and then explore your own answers.

Which three experiences had the most positive impact on you and your life? You might consider family, school, sports, career, entrepreneurship, animals, wilderness /nature, travel to name just a few.

1. _____

2. _____

3. _____

How were you affected by those positive experiences? What did you do differently or how did you change as a result of those experiences?

_____

_____

_____

Which of these experiences would you like to make accessible to others? How could you do that?

_____

_____

_____

What were the top three *negative* life experiences that most affected you?

1. _____

2. _____

3. _____

What impact did they have on your life in the short or long term? How did they change you?

_____

_____

_____

Would you want to help others avoid, or protect others from the same or similar experiences? How could you do this?

_____

_____

_____

In view of your positive and negative life experiences, do you want to help people facing similar challenges and negative situations or do you want to help give others access to the positive experiences that benefited you.

_____

_____

_____

NOTES

_____

_____

_____

_____

_____

_____

_____

_____

_____

_____

_____

_____

_____

_____

_____

_____

_____

_____

The most difficult thing is the decision to act,
the rest is merely tenacity.

— Emelia Earhart

You've done a whole lot of thinking and possibly tapped into some intense emotions, while identifying the life experiences that had the most effect on you. This helped you identify the causes that matter to you and which are mostly likely the ones you'll want to support.

Making the conscious decision to move forward is a defining moment for philanthropy. Consider a massive boulder sitting at the top of a hill. It has "potential energy" that will be released if a certain amount of force is applied to overcome the inertia and get that boulder moving. You've decided you want that rock to roll down the hill, but the decision alone won't move that rock — the action of pushing it will.

Most readers are aware of ABC's television show 20/20, and their "What would you do?" specials. Extreme situations are designed to trigger a spontaneous and often dramatic response from the people witnessing the events which are staged in public settings with actors playing the main characters. Although they don't know they're being filmed for a TV show, most people still don't step in no matter how offended or bothered they might be. In each situation, just a few invariably do speak up or intervene.

I call the first group the *"involved"* because although they're engaged they're not sufficiently motivated when asked. Why didn't you do something? While they found the situation offensive or deeply unsettling, most didn't feel it was dangerous or threatening enough to warrant action. As well, they believe in minding their own business, don't want to risk a confrontation, and don't want to call attention to themselves.

The *"committed"* group explained their almost irresistible compulsion to act in the context of personal connection. They may have related to the individuals because they were once in that situation themselves or they saw someone endure something similar and were determined to prevent a reoccurrence.

Clearly, the *"committed"* group has reconciled the meaning of their life experiences and how they wish to influence change if given the opportunity.

At some point, your desire to do something becomes so overwhelming that you take action.

What typically moves people past the thinking stage and into action? In my experience, most people are motivated by one of these three reasons:

JUSTICE — Righting a situation, punishing offenders, and protecting or saving the affected is often a primary motivator. Regardless of our background, culture, or religion, most of us live by remarkably similar moral and ethical principles around right and wrong. When we witness or experience a contravention of right, we are motivated to seek retribution, or justice in some form, although exactly what form that justice takes is often influenced by our culture and/or religion.

COMPASSION — Compassion and empathy drive action because as discussed earlier, humans connect based on their shared experiences and emotions, then reach out to offer assistance and support where it is needed.

FAITH — The belief that we are all connected by or with a higher power/being gives people a purpose and direction that compels them to reach out to others to share, support, or love.

When you look at your life experiences which one of the above motivations would you have to experience to be compelled to act? Do you see how the six critical life experiences connect?

How will you choose
to help and how do
you select a charity to
support?

"There is no use whatsoever trying to help people who do not help themselves. You cannot push anyone up a ladder unless he is willing to climb himself."

— Andrew Carnegie

————●————————————●————

Once you're motivated to help and prepared to take real action, you have to stop and really think about who you want to help, how you want to help, and exactly what you want the results to be.

Always pick the cause with which you connect on the most profound level.

➤ *That is the first of my five secrets to making a big impact through giving.*

Toward the end of stage one, I asked you to take a long hard look at your life experiences across six categories (family, poverty, affluence, education, physical and mental health/illness/disease, and safety/security), then return to the three most positive, and conversely, negative experiences or moments in your lives. You had to think about how they made you feel and the long-term effects on your character, actions/reactions, and various aspects of your life. To find the cause you're truly passionate about, you had to dig deep.

We then addressed the most powerful and most common motivators — justice, compassion and faith.

As a result, you now have at least one and maybe far more than a few causes that really matter to you particularly when you apply your sense of justice and compassion as well as your need to share with others and support them.

Now, are you absolutely sure that you've found the one cause that will keep you committed and engaged over the long term? You need to find something that really speaks to you to be sure you'll give it the utmost care and attention.

Ask yourself, "If I were able to make a difference for this cause, what would that look like?" What would an organization have to do to help me achieve my philanthropic goals? What are their values? How will they help? Are they effective?

When you absolutely know that you want to promote education, fight poverty, eradicate disease, or save the oceans, I'd recommend you fine tune your focus. Do you want to fund a scholarship for needy girls or teenagers that excel at physics? Do you want to help single moms or farming families that live below the poverty line? How about benefiting animals by providing the funds to neuter or spay dogs?

How do you find a charity that fits your cause of choice? Leverage the power of the internet's extraordinary search engines by plugging in the relevant search terms, then take the time to sift through the organizations and websites that pop up.

Virtually every one of us will be influenced if not swayed one way or the other by the image first presented by the charity's online presence and public image. Remember that building an attractive, user-friendly website that sums up that charity's core message in a few paragraphs and pages is unimaginably easier than actually building and running an effective charity that consistently delivers measurable results to the cause in question.

Look closely at a big philanthropic organization and you will see that it is much like a big business. It might be incredibly well run, but that's not a given, which is why you must execute due diligence before you hand over a dime.

Let's look at homelessness as an example and start with the big picture. If you decide that you want to "end homelessness", you need to recognize that this is a real stretch goal. It's huge and far-reaching because homelessness exists on a global level.

Let's narrow it down. Do want to tackle homelessness in your own city or province? Do you want to reach across Canada or around the world? Is putting a roof over their heads enough or do you want to address the root cause of their homelessness? Do you focus on those who are homeless right now or do you figure out how to keep the next generation from being homeless?

If you decide that affordable housing is the key, you may immediately think of Habitat for Humanity. A well-recognized brand that's lauded for the work it does, Habitat for Humanity may be a good fit but you may also decide that you could provide a "fresh approach and perspective", "strategies and actions".

Time and again, I've seen budding philanthropists with a deep commitment and raging passion decide that they could produce better results if they started from scratch and created a new organization.

While I'd never warn you against launching your own charity, I will point out that you really need to understand the philanthropic landscape and that founding and operating a charity can be even more challenging than running your own company. Why?

As a charity, financial accountability is a major issue and impeccable financial reporting must be a given if you want to maintain your charitable status. Are you really interested in acquiring both the philanthropic and financial expertise required to run your new charity? Can you accept and deal with the fact your actions, personal and professional, will likely be subject to intense public and media scrutiny whether or not they have anything to do with your charity? In fact, in the case of charitable work there is a tendency for moral judgement of executives that holds them to a higher standard than your typical for-profit business leader.

Attracting and raising the capital needed to develop and fund the necessary infrastructure and/or grow the organization requires a different approach. As well, it is invariably a much harder pitch when investors will see social and other intangible benefits, such as a sense of wellbeing, instead of monetary returns.

You should start by asking yourself certain tough questions. Why do I think I can do a better job than existing charities? Why do I really want to start my own charity? Will my charity actually achieve better results? What is the real cost of creating a redundant organization to the cause? Is this about my need for control and/or recognition?

In Canada alone, there are approximately 86,000 registered charities, so I truly believe that if you look, you will find one that is as committed to your cause as you are.

> *Always choose a charity that takes the action(s) required to produce sustainable results for the cause you want to impact.*
>
> ❯❯ *That's the* second of my five secrets *to making a big impact through giving.*

Should you decide to work with an existing philanthropic organization, you want to be sure it supports the very goals that are important to you, but as importantly you need tangible proof that they take the actions required to produce the specified results.

Let's use the City of Calgary, which in 2008 created its "Ten Year Plan to End Homelessness" (by 2018). City leaders and managers recognized that ending homelessness involved much more than providing affordable housing or donating space. To really address the issue long-term, they had to tackle the root causes. To that end, Mayor Nahed Nenshi, and a consortium of experienced local business, community, charity, and social program leaders, including Tim Richter, the president and CEO of the Canadian Alliance to End Homelessness (CAEH) and police chief Rick Hanson shared their observations, experiences and statistical evidence. What were the key learnings?

Many of the homeless had mental health issues, typically the main cause of homelessness, and physical challenges as well as issues relating to illness and addiction. A lack of education and financial resources as well as unstable home environments was also found to have contributed to homelessness.

In the face of so many possible starting points, the City of Calgary team recognized they had to focus on a particular group and agreed to start with the at-risk adults and families who were already without a home.

An interdisciplinary approach was deemed one of several keys to success, so they engaged affordable housing organizations and the police department. Affordable housing can put a roof over someone's head but to keep them under that roof, you need to keep them off the street and out of jail. That can be a significant challenge in the face of mental health, addiction and poverty that can result in violent, criminal, or simply socially unacceptable behavior. If someone is wandering and hearing voices, locking them up doesn't help any more than it does to jail an addict or a mother who stole food to feed her hungry child. In each of these scenarios, the root cause must be identified and addressed as part of a long-term plan that will deliver sustainable results.

If you wanted to help reduce or eliminate homeless in

Calgary or a city like it, what would you do? How would you choose to help?

While your ultimate focus might be homelessness, you may want to step back to address one of its root causes to prevent rather than address homelessness after the fact.

For instance, if someone you know ended up on the street due to poverty resulting from a combination of addictions and mental health issues such as depression or severe anxiety disorder, you could help an organization that supports people with addictions and mental health issues.

> *Always invest the time and effort required to thoroughly research and assess the charity that you have identified as the one that takes the actions required to produce sustainable results for the cause you want to support.*
>
> ▶ *That's the* third *of my five secrets to making a big impact through giving.*

Once you've found the organization and determined that it takes the actions that deliver the results, you're ready for the next steps.

Do you feel good about that charity?

Don't answer that question until you can show me that you've done your due diligence.

Committing to any charity before checking it out is at best naïve, and at worst, irresponsible. It could be akin to pitching your money out the proverbial window.

You'll need to consider and assess their management team, infrastructure, fundraising costs versus funds raised, financial reporting and status, tangible, measurable results, and much more.

Always give the asset that is the most uniquely you; that you have in the greatest abundance and that will most positively impact the charity.

▶ *That* is the fourth of my five secrets to making a big impact through giving.

What should you give? What asset or resource is unique to you and your situation? Every one of us has something to offer, whether it's money, a skill/talent, a public profile, business and personal connections, a resource other than cash such as a cottage that might provide respite to a family with cancer, or the time available to volunteer.

Look at the philanthropic icons such as Oprah, the Gates' and Richard Branson — they're uniquely positioned in that they have every one of those resources and capabilities in extreme abundance, with one exception — time.

Some philanthropists are perfectly content to contribute financially. Others want to become directly involved, because they have a genuine, personal interest in saving polar bears or educating and empowering girls in third-world countries.

However, there are specific points you need to assess when making the decision to become directly involved. It's critical that you first determine what role you want to play and secondly, whether you have the personality/character and relevant skills and experience to make a worthwhile contribution, because if not, you may actually hinder your charity of choice more than you help it move forward.

Always identify and then use the financial tools that are available to protect and preserve your estate, reduce taxes and ultimately maximize the size of the regular and/or final donation(s).

▸ *That is my* **fifth of my five secrets** *to making a big impact through giving.*

Many of you will come to the conclusion that money will be one of your primary gifts to your cause, and as you learned earlier, you can use a variety of tools such as life insurance, stocks or bonds and a donor-advised fund to maximize the funds that will be available to donate and reduce the capital gains tax burden.

Seven Key Characteristics of High-Quality Charities

Now that you've identified the cause that resonates with you and considered the five secrets to big impact giving, I'm going to lead you through a seven-step process that will help you find the high-quality charities that are effective and efficient.

There are seven factors you should assess before becoming involved with a philanthropic organization. If a charity scores well in all seven areas, that is as terrific as it is highly unusual.

In most cases, if a charity scores well in fiduciary duty and prudence, governance and efficiency, which I consider to be of paramount importance when assessing and selecting a charity, they will deliver results if you work with them. A high score in each of fiduciary duty and prudence, governance and efficiency ensures the charity will carefully manage, track, and report on the funds it receives and use them in a way that delivers the biggest impact to the people and cause you and they intend to help.

Transparency, accessibility, and freedom of information also warrant your close attention because they will reflect the organization's culture as well as the attitudes and behavior of senior managers and board members.

Assess each characteristic and assign it a score of one to five points with one as the lowest and five as the top rating.

If a charity scores less than three, particularly in either fiduciary duty and prudence, governance or efficiency, I would strongly suggest you stop the investigative process and look at another charity.

In order of priority, let's get started:

1. Fiduciary duty and prudence. A fiduciary is an individual who is entrusted to act in the best interests of the organization with both integrity and honesty. Fiduciary duty and prudence are about management's decision-making process as it relates to the investment and granting of capital and financial resources. As stewards of the public's trust, philanthropic organizations must demonstrate fiduciary duty and prudence in everything that they do. Specifically in the areas of the acquisition of funds, the allocation of funds and the types of assets in which they invest, and the disbursement of funds from the capital or investments for operations or to charities/causes that are supported.

*The CRA has set a minimum disbursement amount for endowment capital at 3.5% annually.

How do you know if they truly understand the importance of their roles as fiduciaries and the requirements? If they can accurately define fiduciary and can demonstrate an understanding of their role in the decision-making process, it's a positive indicator. As one example, a member of the investment committee must play a fiduciary role, while the treasurer who tracks the funds doesn't as he has no say in how the funds are invested or spent.

Score: _____ out of five

Charities are stewards of the public trust, in the form of capital. Those organizations with no understanding of their important role as fiduciaries will be less likely to properly manage the funds entrusted to them.

2. Governance. Governance is a critical issue. It deals with how an organization operates on the inside and is a principles-based function that is closely aligned with transparency and access. Principles-based decision-making

is all about taking action based on what is right. While the principles and actions will reflect the rules and policies, rules-based management tends to be more rigid and can put rules and regulations ahead of the overall mission. In a rules-based scenario, management asks "Is this allowed?" and "Is this restricted?" instead of "Why?" and "Is this the right thing to do to meet our goals?"

The organization should follow best practices in dealing with both day-to-day issues and the long-term achievement of the goals of the organization. There should be a strong policy about oversight to prevent such problems as self-dealing.

Without proper governance in place, organizations are exposed to so many potential pitfalls ranging from financial dealings, to conflicts, to mandate drift.

Score: _____ out of five

3. EFFICIENCY: In the non-profit world, charities have learned that they must use their resources efficiently — from the financial to the human — in order to maximize their impact. In my experience, non-profit organizations typically do a far better job than most government agencies.

When assessing efficiency:

1. What percentage of the funds raised/available is used to help the cause or people for which it is intended? This will vary significantly for each charity but the CRA does consider a charity's fundraising ratio and will look at it more closely if it falls outside certain parameters.

2. If the ratio of costs to revenue over a certain fiscal period is under 35%, the CRA is unlikely to question it or investigate further.

3. If the ratio of costs to revenue over a certain fiscal period is 35% and higher, the CRA will examine the average ratio over recent years to determine whether there has been an increase in fundraising costs. The higher the ratio, and the greater the recent increase in costs, the greater the likelihood the CRA will demand a detailed accounting of the expenditures.

4. If the ratio of costs to revenue over a certain fiscal period is above 70%, the CRA is going to insist on a detailed explanation and rationale. For the CRA and for you, this is a huge red flag!

5. What percentage of funds raised/available covers operational costs or infrastructure, including office space, staff salaries, marketing and promotion?

6. What percentage of funds raised/available is spent on fundraising, whether it is mail campaigns, special events, etc.? Does the ratio of money spent to fundraise versus the money raised make sense?

Score: _____ out of five

4. TRANSPARENCY: In most cases, it is ideal to exhibit true transparency around a charity's finances, operations, fund-raising, and cause-oriented results indicates integrity, superior management, and efficacy.

When assessing transparency:

1. Can you access their financials or an annual report?

2. Can you see hierarchical structures and the various individuals/positions' responsibilities?

3. Where does their money come from? Where exactly does it go and when?

4. Exactly how have they helped their cause and over what time periods? What are the tangible, measurable results?

Score: _____ out of five

In my experience, a lack of transparency in any of these areas is a red flag that suggests they are hiding information because it would reflect poorly on them. If you learn that the organization is hiding information or making it too hard to access, I would recommend that you walk away.

If there is a lack of transparency because they don't recognize the importance and value of gathering the information, putting it into an accessible, easily understood format and making it available, it's truly unfortunate. Making the effort and not realizing the true value of those actions because someone didn't know a report was needed, didn't know how to prepare a report, or simply couldn't be bothered suggests a fundamental lack of operational, communications, and business acumen and experience.

Could the necessary skills and processes be acquired? Of course, but it's not your job to tell them why transparency is important or what they need to do to achieve it.

I would suggest you move on!

5. ACCESSIBILITY AND FREEDOM OF INFORMATION: An organization should be willing to provide access to information and documentation and as a donor, I would strongly suggest that you weigh the value of your potential donation against your requests for access and information. In short, the more you're willing to give, the more information and access you require to justify and protect your eventual decision and your funds.

A gift of $1,000, $10,000, or $100,000 requires significant amounts of information and access!

Keep in mind that a registered charity must provide and regularly update their financial information on the Canada Revenue Agency Charity website, which means the information is already out there and available to the public at large.

You can expect to easily obtain minutes and bylaws from the charity and they should be willing to share information on their governance and policies.

However, it's unrealistic to expect open and timely access to "in-camera" sessions or personnel and operations decisions. Open access and freedom of information is so important that I would advise against working with an organization that doesn't embrace it. Being able to communicate directly with the key players and access information is always a good thing.

If they are reluctant to share minutes and memoranda of board or executive meetings, ask yourself why they are being cagey and secretive.

Score: _____ out of five

6. FINANCIAL NEED: An organization should be capable of communicating its needs in a variety of ways in order to be effective in both raising money and following its mission.

As an example, if Habit for Humanity wants to fulfill its mission of building ten affordable homes, it will explain that it needs $2 million to acquire the land, permits, materials and more.

While it is assumed all organizations will require financial assistance of some sort, think back to one of my first examples and ask whether they need it to pay the rent, the phone bill, or staff salaries? Is it required to support a fundraising event that will ultimately benefit the cause or simply warrant coverage in the society or entertainment pages?

Score: _____ out of five

7. SIMPLICITY. An organization should have a simple hierarchical structure so they are able to implement actions and make decisions fairly quickly. If there are multiple, complex layers, it will take too much time and effort to navigate the red tape while the number of senior and mid-level executives, staff and volunteers is also sure to be reflected in the operational costs.

If an organization's goal is to provide emergency food sources, but it has the structure of a government agency, chances are it will be unable to make the necessary decisions as quickly as is required to get food to hungry people in a timely or cost-effective manner.

Score: _____ out of five

Add up the scores for each category to determine the charity's final ranking so that you can take the next step in the selection process, but remember that fiduciary duty and prudence, governance and efficiency are the most important characteristics, followed by transparency, accessibility, freedom of information, and financial need.

#1 Score:	_____	#5 Score:	_____
#2 Score:	_____	#6 Score:	_____
#3 Score:	_____	#7 Score:	_____
#4 Score:	_____	TOTAL:	_____

If an organization receives a total score of 29 to 35, you have an all-star! This organization really knows what it takes to make a difference, operate well, and will likely have incredible impact in all they do.

If an organization receives a total score of 22 to 28, then you should seriously look at them. They have a lot of things going for them and generally "get it". It is likely any shortcomings result more from a lack of resources than a lack of relevant skills, experience or understanding.

If an organization receives a total score of 15 to 21, you can still consider them; however you need to know that they will likely have to work as much on their own infrastructure, processes, and governance as their cause, possibly more.

If an organization receives a total score of 0 to 14, then I'd strongly suggest that you walk away from them.

I would like to see donors work with charities that have earned scores of at least 22 and up. If a lower score is indicated, then it is likely money and effort will used be internally for as much, if not more than for their beneficiaries in support of their respective causes.

When pondering their low scores and your next move, ask yourself whether any of them fit into the six "dysfunctional" categories outlined below.

SIX DYSFUNCTIONAL CHARITIES TO WATCH OUT FOR

Every year, close to 1,600 charities have their charitable status revoked by Revenue Canada because they have violated certain parameters, so you need to be aware of the most common issues so that you can watch for them. Some are immediately obvious, others are a little more subtle, but the onus is on you to protect your interests by avoiding the dysfunctional charities in favour of the high-quality organizations.

THE INEFFICIENT ORGANIZATION:

At the first and even third or fourth glance, this charity looks great because their good intentions, work ethic, ability to engage stakeholders, and even their results are so impressive they make potential donors feel warm and fuzzy. However, a number of these charities are burdened by redundancy that results in the highly ineffective use of its often abundant resources. Why or how does this happen? They may be understaffed or their staff may be as unqualified as they are passionate and dedicated. Conversely, they may have too many experienced, skilled staff working on tasks that don't fully utilize their expertise. Support this organization and you will see superficial results, you will at least initially feel good, but eventually, you will understand that your funds could have accomplished far more elsewhere.

THE ALL-SIZZLE, NO-SUBSTANCE CHARITY:

Great branding puts the organization front and center. While that's the reality, it is unfortunate when donors fund the biggest, shiniest, most headline-grabbing charities regardless of how they actually impact the cause they support. We've all seen the flashy fundraising campaigns, the heart-wrenching TV ads, the sophisticated high-tech websites, and the celebrity-dotted events for the trendy issues that are making headlines and trending on Twitter today. Look at the cost of the efforts in relation to the funds actually raised and you may need to dig deeper then look away because the all-sizzle, no-substance charity also has a "waste" culture around administrative, marketing, promotional, and operational costs.

THE CONFLICTED CHARITY:

Founders, senior managers, and stakeholders have typically invested plenty of time and money, which is appealing to investors and donors who assume that the personal stakes involved will ensure prudent financial stewardship. There is truth in this; however conflict can arise when key stakeholders find that their need to manage their personal risk conflicts with the charity's original goals. The same potential for conflict can also come into play when a donor is also a director who pushes his or her own agenda and discounts the opinions and advice of others. It's also worth noting that while strong leadership is a benefit, it is important that the organization has a structure and a plan that provide stability and direction when transitioning to new leader(s), otherwise it can negatively affect continuity, vision, relationships, and more.

THE INEFFECTIVE ORGANIZATION:

An ineffective organization is entirely different from an inefficient organization, because it never completes tasks needed to produce results. Their ideas and plans are typically big and exciting, which again lures donors, but the team lacks the skills to execute, implement, and see anything through to completion. You will want to help, but you need to realize your efforts and money will be wasted.

The outright scam:

These so-called charities are the reason that nearly 1,600 of them have their status revoked annually. Yes, I know I mentioned such charities just four paragraphs above — but it bears repeating.

You are almost sure to spot the scam charity if you've diligently assessed the seven characteristics of high-quality charities as scammers tend to be oblivious or willfully ignorant of fiduciary duty and prudence, governance, transparency, accessibility, and freedom of information. They are highly likely to withhold and guard information, discourage or even block access to financials and staff, cannot demonstrate an efficient use of funds, and don't clearly communicate their financial need(s).

As a result, it's also possible the information they've provided to the CRA's charity website is lacking or outdated and that the CRA has asked for details and explanations on their ratio of costs to revenue information.

In addition, if the tax deductions, grants, results, actions, or anything else seems too good to be true — it's a sure sign that plenty of further investigation is required although you could save yourself time by walking away immediately.

"I'm not really sure WHAT they do" charity:

On so many levels, this organization exhibits the most important if not all seven of the seven characteristics of high-quality charities, yet the fact their mission is too broad or misleading is a major red flag. "Helping humanity" or "serving our children and families" is admirable and will connect with most individuals' values, but the lack of focus on a specific problem renders them ineffective. If you don't have a very clearly defined goal, how can you develop and implement the actions required to attain it?

You determine your unique approach to your philanthropy, but you owe it to yourself and the years you've invested in building and growing your estate to thoroughly research and investigate the charities that interest you to ensure the maximum impact. To really drive significant, sustainable change — you need to do your homework.

How will you maximize
your skills and unique
abilities to leverage your
impact?

"Strive not to be a success, but rather to be of value."

— Albert Einstein

●────────── ──────────●

As we move through our lives, we typically strive for what we consider success or achievement, which we may define differently for ourselves and for others. We also recognize that how we define success and achievement may evolve or even change drastically based on our life experiences.

If we're successful, chances are we've become aware of our best and most unique abilities and used them to our advantage. Understanding our strengths, or unique abilities, and knowing how to leverage them will determine our success, whether we're independent professionals, senior executives with private or public firms, or business owners and entrepreneurs. We typically love what we're good at because it feels right and while it still requires effort, it's a whole different kind of effort than that required to pursue something we're not inherently interested in or good at.

Successful musicians, athletes, actors, scientists, entrepreneurs, and CEOs all know early on what they're passionate about and what they excel at. When they focus exclusively on their greatest strengths and vigorously and passionately pursue them, they rise to the top.

Einstein once said: *"Everyone is a genius. But if you judge a fish on its ability to climb a tree, it will live its whole life believing that it is stupid."*

Why aren't we using our best talents? In some cases, it's because we're not completely clear about what our unique abilities really are, or it may be because we'd rather be something other than what we really are.

At some point in our lives, most of us were told to devote ourselves to getting better at the things for which we lacked a natural aptitude and in which we weren't particularly interested. For some of us, it was math, science or physics, for others it might have been English and history, or even sports, music or art.

Why? It was believed it would build character, develop diligence and perseverance, and teach us to be team players, show us how to work alone, and/or inspire creativity and innovation.

If you knew exactly what you were good at and were clear about what really challenged you, you had a pretty good idea what you should be doing. However, if you tended to be pretty good at a lot of things, you might do a little bit of everything.

Through high school and university, I was truly a jack of all trades and master of none. Back then, no one taught me the value or showed me the wisdom of identifying, then further developing and leveraging my strongest attributes with single-minded passion and energy.

Some of us figure it out on our own, but that can be almost impossible when parents, teachers, and coaches are telling us to try everything and then do our best to get better at what we're bad at.

Today, we're all expected to know enough about our cars and our technology to either troubleshoot the problem or monitor those charged with the repairs. We turn to "Dr. Google" to self-diagnose and rely on whatever the search engines turn up for everything from medical expertise to financial advice. A little bit of knowledge can work for us, but it can also lead us in the wrong direction and result in ill-advised decisions.

"I can do things you cannot; you can do things I cannot; together we can do great things."

— Mother Teresa

This focus on our passions and unique abilities applies as much to our philanthropic endeavors as it does to our lives and careers. We need to work just as hard, if not harder, to identify what we can best contribute to a philanthropic organization as we did to leverage our unique abilities to best serve our own careers and businesses.

While we want to work with philanthropic leaders who are as passionate and driven as we are, we still have to focus on the tools and strategies we'll use to maximize our financial and other contributions.

Look at iconic philanthropists and consider how they're using their unique abilities and positioning. Oprah Winfrey is an outstanding example of someone who truly understands her greatest strengths and strategically leverages them in both her business and philanthropic endeavors.

Early on, Oprah Winfrey made a tidal shift in her career and set the tone for her enormous success when she decided to focus on helping others through her daytime talk show. To do good, she consciously committed to avoiding the sensationalist negativity her competitors promoted. Her strategic, soul-based decision changed the course of television talk shows and media history.

Understandably, we focus most on Oprah's wealth which Forbes estimates at almost $3 billion. No doubt, Oprah Winfrey's wealth is an extraordinary tool, but her ability to reach and influence a massive audience also has a powerful impact. As just one example, Oprah's deep commitment to reading, her focus on the value of reading, and her joy in it, have helped make literacy a priority across the U.S. and elsewhere while ensuring a love and acceptance of reading and books.

Oprah continues to guide and lead her media empire while allowing others to run her charities.

In life, business and philanthropy, our strengths are

meaningful and impactful only when we do something with them.

Philanthropically, all of our Big Impact Giving actions fall within these categories:

➤ MONEY

➤ TIME

➤ INFLUENCE

GIVING MONEY

All charities require capital to pay for programs, people and services as well as marketing, office space and operating costs, so of course, financial donations are of paramount importance.

Tangible gifts include everything from cash to investment assets, land, buildings, products, goods, services, and more. Their value can range from the loonie dropped into the Salvation Army Christmas kettle to the multi-million dollar endowment.

How do you decide how much to give? According to Ipsos Reid's "Philanthropy in Canada, 2008 Survey" and the Fraser Research Bulletin in 2013, on average Canadians give 1% of their net income, while Americans tend to contribute 2%, although the generally accepted standard or guideline, often used by religious organizations, is in fact 10%. So it's fair to say the range is 1% to 10%, although when one is given, the average bequest from an estate is 20% of the estate's assets for those who give to charity.

Every individual is different but to start, look at how much of your income you need to support your current lifestyle and the way you wish to live upon your retirement. As well, you likely want to consider what and/or how much you want to leave to your heirs. Once you have determined the amount required to support your current and retirement lifestyle and leave what you feel is appropriate to your heirs, you will be left with the surplus assets or income, which you can then re-direct to charity to protect it from threats such as taxes. When planning ahead, remember that you're working with what you consider your surplus wealth.

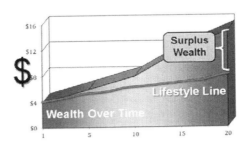

As importantly, you want to think about whether you want to make an annual donation of $1,500, for example, over the course of decades or turn that annual donation into a one-time $500,000 donation through planned giving to maximize the ultimate impact.

Financial contributions are typically direct and relatively simple without the emotions that can accompany a more personal commitment and involvement.

Today, charities have discovered and successfully employed new fund-raising tools such as crowd-funding, which uses the internet and social media to source relatively small amounts of cash from multiple sources and pool it for a particular purpose. They also use micro-loan programs, which extend very small loans to individuals and groups that wouldn't typically qualify for traditional loans. However, many organizations and donors continue to rely on more traditional cash donation tools, including cash and securities (stocks), as the primary source of funds.

Giving time

As people consider their lives, regardless of age, most wish they had spent more time with family and friends and doing the things that they love and that matter most to them. Few, if any, will tell you that they should have worked harder or devoted more hours to their companies and careers to make even more money.

Every single person, regardless of their position in life, has the same 24 hours a day, seven days of the week. Most people, as they move through life, will realize that their time is a valuable and precious commodity precisely because it is scarce and finite. Try as we might, we can't make more time; we can only better manage and allocate the time that we do have.

What we do with that time defines us, and how much time you give to a non-profit organization is worth careful consideration, as is what you will do to help.

While you can ask a non-profit to create a volunteer position that's specifically tailored to your needs in terms of scheduling and preferred tasks, this approach won't serve you or the organization.

Why? This strategy reflects your needs and your skills — it has nothing to do with what the non-profit really needs to achieve its desired results.

To ensure the organization, the cause, the beneficiaries, and the volunteers experience the best and maximum impact, the identification of the need must precede the creation of the role and "job" description. Once that has been achieved, the organization, like any business, can start searching for the people who can fill those positions. Astute managers and executives avoid developing roles to meet the needs of any individual.

In most cases, I suggest you approach the non-profit and ask them about the range of volunteer roles and positions that are available, then decide how your skills, expertise, and experience might be used.

How much time are you willing to invest in coaching, mentoring, or in an advisory role? What is a realistic weekly or monthly commitment? Are you prepared to show up on a consistent, long-term basis?

While the amount of "free" time you have available is obviously a key factor, it is crucial you select a cause that you really care about. As a volunteer, you're not getting paid, so your reward comes in knowing that you are helping support a cause you care deeply about, and in which you have a genuine interest.

A single parent may not have time or money to spare, but some will be able to influence those in their communities. A student is likely in a similar financial position but has the energy, enthusiasm, and time, while a baby boomer may have money, time, and influence.

What are your unique skills or personality traits?

Which of those skills would most benefit what type of organization?

If you want to leverage specific expertise, you could help coach young athletes with an interest in sports such as hockey and baseball, soccer and football, or even track and field, skiing, sailing, and rowing. You may be able to offer guidance and training in the arts (painting, music, theatre, creative writing) or in business (finance, human resources, marketing, PR, information technology).

However, you may recognize that your "soft" skills could be better suited to mentoring and coaching young people who need to further develop life and relationship skills, or serving as a Big Brother or Big Sister.

If you have the time, but can't find the right fit for your skills, you could help out with community cleanups, chauffeur people who can't drive, deliver meals to seniors, or serve soup — the need, and the opportunities, are unlimited.

Volunteering with an organization can be incredibly rewarding but it can also prove profoundly challenging. If you're expecting an environment that is as predictable and structured as the typical workplace, or if your commitment depends on the show of appreciation and the accolades received, you might need to reconsider your suitability as a volunteer.

Volunteering in a hospice, a home that provides a hotel alternative to parents with very sick children, or a shelter for abused women or animals is sure to take an emotional toll.

Are you prepared to deal with the fallout and how will you handle it?

Chairing an event or a board is demanding in terms of time, focus, and energy, but it can also be a challenge to manage a group of diverse, passionate, committed individuals who will test your diplomatic skills and people management abilities.

Worldwide, non-profits, churches, sports teams, bands, associations and communities are able to help others due in large part to the individuals and collectives who make volunteering a vital, rewarding part of their lives.

In 2010 in Canada alone, baby boomers and senior adults contributed over a billion hours to non-profits — that's over $10 billion worth of equivalent paid time at minimum wage and it is worth remembering that most of these individuals would typically be paid *much* more based on their skills, expertise, and experience.

To learn more about volunteering and older adults in Canada, you can visit

▶ http://volunteer.ca/content/volunteering-and-older-adults-final-report (http://bit.do/TMfZ)

GIVING INFLUENCE

Every one of us has the ability to influence others but some are infinitely more powerful influencers because of our drive, initiative, character, life experience, circumstances, and an innate ability to lead others.

While we typically think of high-profile individuals who are prominent in the political, business, sports, and celebrity worlds as the most influential, there are many noteworthy exceptions. Let's look at a few influencers who had little, if any social status and limited, or even non-existent financial means, but whose actions really did change the world by increasing our awareness, inspiring our support, and compelling us to give.

Would you help raise money for cancer because of a celebrity such as Angelina Jolie or because a colleague, close friend, or family member had been affected by the disease?

We need to be moved by people, situations, and stories that are somehow familiar or they connect with our sense of what's truly right or profoundly wrong.

In January 2009, the Taliban said that no Pakistani girl would be allowed to go to school and at that time, an 11-year-old Pakistani girl named Malala Yousafzai asked: 'Why should we be silent? Why don't we speak up for our rights? Why don't we tell the world what is happening in Swat.'

Malala did not want the Swat Valley where she grew up to become the next Afghanistan, so she started blogging for the BBC. Under a pseudonym, she wrote about her love of learning, the Taliban oppression, and especially the ban on education for girls in Swat.

She recognized that her story mattered beyond her own country's borders and understood that it would resonate globally. Men, women, girls, and boys were moved and motivated worldwide.

Although the Taliban's reach and control continued to

expand, Malala and her father didn't back down despite the threats against Malala, her father, and their entire family. One summer day, while riding the bus home from school, two young men stopped the bus, boarded and asked "Who is Malala?"

They took aim and shot 14-year-old Malala in front of her schoolmates leaving her for dead. A single bullet hit the left side of her left eye, then travelled down through her shoulder.

Not only did Malala recover after nearly dying, , she was awarded a Nobel Prize for her continued global crusade for girls' rights and education, which has helped her connect with world leaders who also have the power to influence.

Our influence is often the most powerful when our story and actions are highly personal, but the more personal our story, the more challenging and risky it can be.

For Malala and other influencers, death threats and attempted assassinations and attacks are an issue, but even if the stakes aren't as high for other influencers, they may not want to subject their public persona to further scrutiny, jeopardize their income, or alter their position in a particular community.

The role of influencer can attract the positive but it can also have a negative impact.

Before you take on the role of influencer, you need to consider how your influence can be used to benefit your cause, but you also want to think about how that role could affect you and your family on a day to day basis.

When donors identify and leverage their best attributes, whether that contribution is made in the form of money, time, influence or a combination thereof, there are four mistakes that even the most well-intentioned donors invariably make. Once you're aware of them, you're better able to avoid them.

TOP 4 MISTAKES
IN GIVING TO A CHARITABLE ORGANIZATION:

TREATING A NON-PROFIT OR CHARITY AS A FOR-PROFIT:
While most charities will benefit when managed as businesses, there are significant differences that must be considered. As I mentioned earlier, charities must respect and abide by stringent reporting rules to maintain their charitable status or not-for-profit standing. To qualify as a charity that can issue tax credits to donors, the organization must direct as much of the revenue or "profit" to the cause and its people as possible rather than using the funds to support projects that don't directly impact either one. Individuals who are accustomed to working in the for-profit sector will need to look at profitability differently in the non-profit world, and recognize that its long-term existence, growth, and social impact are at least as important.

As in any business, sustainability is crucial at a non-profit, but it has to be balanced with the return for the charity's beneficiaries. Over the years, I've seen for-profit executives struggle with what they see as a real conflict between sustainability and the flow through beneficiary funding in the non-profit sector, which can be a strain for both the donor and the organization's management team.

The size of the profit, where and when those profits are directed, and the issue of sustainability often set the board of directors, who represent the donors, and the executive staff, who stand for the beneficiaries, against one another despite the fact that their respective goals are actually remarkably similar deep down. Reconciling a near- or short-term — return on investment (profit) with the long-term social return on investment (impact) will always be a challenge, particularly when the change in the beneficiaries' circumstances may not be readily apparent combined with the fact they rarely, if ever, tangibly demonstrate their appreciation.

If you're unable or unwilling to adapt to the non-profit world, you may need to think about whether you will be an effective and accepted volunteer, donor, or leader as well as how changing your approach and behavior will sit with you over the long term.

MORE MONEY BUT MINIMAL RETURN:

People often donate money because it's simpler and cleaner than contributing time or influence, but a well-considered financial contribution has its own set of issues.

How much money is enough? There is no easy answer to that question, but I can tell you that more money, or even any money may not be the answer. Before you commit any funds, you need to look into the organization and the results it has achieved with its funds. If the "returns" or social impact is not in line with the investment, you need to look at donating your money to another cause.

ASSUMING THERE'S NO BUSINESS IN THE NON-PROFIT BUSINESS:

A charity that is effective and efficient, while consistently achieving its goals and delivering the required results typically does so because it is capably managed as a business.

In a non-profit, the executive staff generally has more of a socially-driven educational background with a focus on the social, psychological, or scientific rather than a business, economics, or finance orientation. Their skill set is well-suited to serving their beneficiaries but there can be a gap with it comes to operational decisions and strategic planning.

As a result, the non-profit's executive staff may look to the board's directors and advisers for their business acumen and their problem-solving abilities.

While their ideas on exactly how to run the organization may differ — sometimes drastically — there are as many inherent advantages as there are challenges.

Because some of those goals and results are a challenge to quantify or measure, and simply because the organizations are referred to as non-profits or charities, they are not seen as a business, which I frankly find ludicrous.

While the perception is that a charity is not profit-oriented, it is vital that the charity produce a "profit" or surplus. The difference is the "profit" or surplus is directed to the cause and its people rather than to the owners, shareholders, and stakeholders.

The profit-at-all-costs just won't work in any charity or social enterprise, but there still has be an appropriate mix of business and charity.

IGNORING THE BUSINESS ASPECTS OF NON-PROFITS:

If one assumes there is no business in the non-profit business, then it stands to reason that donors and management will not apply themselves in a businesslike manner or be expected to run as a fiscally prudent business. As I've already stated, there are differences, but on a fundamental level a non-profit and for-profit still share many characteristics and principles.

Astute managers and executives who run their non-profits according to business fundamentals will likely generate remarkable results and have a significant impact on their beneficiaries.

Blake Mycoskie, entrepreneur, philanthropist, and founder of TOMS Shoes, struck an extraordinary balance between the for-profit and non-profit worlds. While travelling in Argentina in 2006, Blake saw how many children were growing up without shoes, and decided to create a for-profit business with a charitable twist. His "One for One" business model ensured that for every TOMS shoe sold, a person that needed shoes would get a pair free of charge. Since 2006, TOMS has given more than 10 million pairs of shoes to children and his TOMS Eyewear program has helped more than 175,000 individuals with new glasses since 2011.

His unique blend of style, kitsch and do-good philanthropy with highly visible, tangible results came together to create phenomenal financial success.

Blake made giving a part of his "One for One" business model and increasingly charities are making business a part of the non-profit model because it ensures they can do more for their beneficiaries.

While you can see it as a business created to fund philanthropy, others may see it as a sustainable charitable organization that was set up and run as a business that generates its own revenues to ensure both its ability to support its primary causes and do it indefinitely.

TOMS' brilliant business model is effective and sustainable — so why don't more businesses or charities embrace similar strategies?

Doing something so far from what is expected in the business and charitable worlds really requires a unique vision and an innate sense of daring as well as an ability to accept the inherent risks.

Habitat for Humanity is another outstanding example of just how non-profit and for-profit efforts can coexist within the same organization to everyone involved. In the beginning, Habitat for Humanity relied on donations to secure the funds to buy land, then plan and build new and affordable homes for deserving families. They typically required cash to acquire the land, but the materials were often donated, and the labor was provided by volunteers.

Post-build, Habitat for Humanity found it was often left with excess materials, equipment, and tools that for whatever reason weren't required for their next build. As a result, the organization created its ReStore retail business to sell these products to consumers. Over time, ReStore evolved and began accepting retail overstock, end-of-line products and donated items for resale. The resulting profits were then re-directed back into the Habitat for Humanity in the community in which that ReStore operated. Thanks to the ReStore model, Habitat for Humanity has access to more cash and will be more viable over the long-term. In the face of changing circumstances, Habitat for Humanity recognized the potential opportunities and adapted its business model to leverage them.

Taking action:
WHAT WILL YOU DO?

*"Whatever you do will be insignificant,
but it is very important that you do it."*

— Mahatma Gandhi

———————————————

Mahatma Gandhi firmly believed that one person can change the world and that one person could influence another and so on, to exponentially increase the power and reach of the individual.

Gandhi's "small" acts of nonviolent civil disobedience eventually became a national movement, led India to independence from Britain, and inspired civil rights and freedom initiatives around the world. Likewise, African-American civil rights activist and seamstress Rosa Parks violated a city ordinance at the age of 42, defiantly sitting in the "whites only" section of the bus and refusing to give up her seat to a white passenger. She was arrested and fined, but her action inspired a movement that fuelled others and would eventually lead to the end of legal segregation in America.

In the right context, at the right time, small, seemingly "insignificant" acts that require great courage really can challenge and eventually change deeply-held beliefs and eventually political and legal systems.

What will you do? What action will you take?

The philanthropic journey is much like a road trip! We've done the research and the pre-planning. We've figured out what matters to us and where we want to go as a result. We've cleared our schedules and planned our route. We've decide which vehicle is best suited to this particular geography and destination. At last, we're ready to get into that driver's seat and hit the road. At some point, we have to get beyond thinking about it and planning it, in order to take action. In 1988, Nike launched its "Just Do It!" marketing campaign, which inspired generations of jocks, athletes, and fitness wannabes as well as people who embraced it as a mantra for living. Those three little words, "Just Do It", continue to inspire and resonate.

I'm committed to helping Canadians pass their wealth from one generation to the next, protect their assets from various threats (mostly taxes), preserve their legacies, and I want to you to "just do it" sooner rather than later.

Why? What drives me?

In my case — the question should be "Who drives you?"

My answer: "Judy" and her husband "Frank"!

They were much-loved family friends who sporadically flew into our lives to spread joy and share their boundless energy and enthusiasm. As long as I knew "Judy", I saw her as a 70 something with an outlandish personality and a passion for horse-racing in a red polka-dotted blouse tucked into perfectly pressed, blue polyester pants. Always animated, Judy's face invariably got an extra boost from her brilliant blue eye shadow and bright red L'Oreal lipstick. Judy was the star while Frank was perfectly comfortable playing the supporting role.

By the time Frank died, I was an investment advisor who was surprised that our apparently eccentric family friends had also been astute real estate investors with significant RRSP holdings. I was concerned for Judy's future and financial security. Of course, I offered my help as an advisor and naturally, Judy indulged me.

I put my advisor hat on and immediately charged into problem solving mode. As a start, I told Judy she should "set up a family trust and buy an annuity"... she just stared blankly at me. Judy, ever polite, simply thanked me and said she'd stick with the advice her accountant, of twenty years, had provided her and Frank. It was clear I had jumped ahead and pushed a solution on her rather than listening more closely to what she wanted.

Years later, I was consulting with families to manage their wealth and plan their finances, as well as speaking and writing about these topics. Out of the blue, Judy called. We met to discuss what was important to her and what she could do to ensure her wishes would become a reality after she was gone. We made a good start and while I knew her estate would face some serious challenges down the road, Judy promised we'd wrap it all up when she returned a few months later.

Unfortunately, Judy took ill and died before we'd taken any concrete action. While our family had lost a great friend, I suspected that was not all that had been lost. Once her estate had been settled, she owed the Canada Revenue Agency almost $700,000 in taxes which left significantly less than expected for her heirs!!

I was furious and blamed the government, but the CRA was simply enforcing the tax code. Procrastination, a lack of knowledge and planning were the true culprits.

If contemplating your own mortality can be uncomfortable, discussing how your death will affect your estate and your heirs can be downright difficult, but it has to be done. Are you comfortable leaving the bulk of your estate to all Canadians through the CRA or would you rather have that money go to your heirs and the causes/non-profits that truly matter to you?

Because of my experiences and those of people like Judy and Frank, I want to help people just like you do whatever is necessary to preserve their estates for their heirs and ensure their legacy is fully realized after they're gone.

As an investment and philanthropic consultant with a commitment to continuous learning, I had been speaking in Toronto at a conference and an acquaintance of mine recommended I take a closer look at a program to connect with charities and their donors. It was then that I discovered the Donor Motivation Program™, an elegant and effective approach that serves charities while educating donors and engaging them in discussions of legacy giving. The founder of the program was Scott Keffer, of Pittsburgh, PA. Scott later became an instrumental business coach and mentor of mine. The Donor Motivation Program™ fundamentally changed the way I speak with donors and charities about planned giving. Over the years, I've incorporated a variety of best practices into my own legacy planning process, which I've continued to refine and grow year to year for nearly two decades.

During this time, I've worked with hundreds of men and women to make estate planning meaningful and help them realize a bigger impact in their lives. When individuals or their advisors lack the specific, relevant knowledge and expertise as well as the appropriate tools, they tend to repeat the same mistakes.

Once you're aware of the seven most common estate-planning and giving mistakes, I hope you'll be able to avoid them.

The Top 7 Mistakes in Giving

1. Leaving an RRSP or RRIF to Your Heirs

Both the RRSP and RRIF are excellent long-term tax-sheltered savings vehicles for the owners of those funds while they are still living. However, when the last spouse or sole owner of the plan dies, the entire value of an RRSP or RRIF will be treated as income in deceased's final tax return. For example, an Albertan who died with a $500,000 RRIF would be considered to have an additional income of $500,000 in the year that he died. As a result, his estate would owe the CRA up to $195,000! In provinces other than Alberta, the tax consideration might be as high as 42%.

2. Not considering your legacy

My grandmother was a beautiful kind-hearted woman and when she died at 97 in 2012, her great-grandchildren knew her well. They knew what she stood for and they knew her first name. Can you say that about your great grandmother? When I ask audiences that very question, I am always astounded by how few people actually raise their hands. Most people don't even know the first name of the woman who made their very existence possible! My children understand exactly who Ida June Martin was and what she stood for. As you contemplate your charitable giving, you must ponder your legacy. I ask people to look at their legacy through the eyes of their grandchildren. When we see it from our beneficiaries' perspective, we're often better able to see how what we do today shapes the impact of our giving.

3. Giving through taxation
— involuntary philanthropy

Whether or not most Canadians realize it, and frankly, the vast majority don't have a clue, we tend to support our countrymen primarily through our capital gains and income taxes, which can be up to 42% of a high earning individual's annual income. Yet, not even the most powerful, influential individual has a say in how the government spends that money or who benefits from it.

We recognize we'd more efficiently and strategically direct our wealth than our government does and it's highly likely we'd support causes other than those chosen by the government.

Fortunately, our government incentivizes and promotes voluntary philanthropy through the tax-free gifting of securities and other tax credits for charitable donations. We have been given the means to control how we direct our social capital; we must explore every way we can do this.

4. Failing to Maximize the Size of the Gift

As you learned earlier, people can often give far more to charity than they ever thought possible, if they work with a specialist who has the relevant financial expertise and understands planned giving. Plan strategically, use the right tools and you will pay less tax and have more to give.

5. Focusing on the Wrong Metrics

When investigating a charity, some donors hone in on the expense ratio or even the chairman of the board, but to know if that organization will use the donor's funds to maximize impact, you need to ask about the charity's overall results as they relate to their primary mission.

6. Giving the wrong gift at the wrong time

Deciding to make an impactful gift is the first step. The second is to maximize the impact both for the charity you wish to support, and for your financial circumstances. Reviewing your financial, tax, and estate planning will identify opportunities in maximizing your gift's impact. Do you give now or give through your estate? How can you make your current surplus cash flow do more? There are ways to give much more of what would otherwise be a small annual gift. Review your personal circumstances and then consult a professional advisor to ensure you're fully aware of the benefits of future or planned giving over current giving.

7. Not seeking the most relevant professional help

Establishing a relationship with a client-centred professional who is an expert in planned giving is crucial to successful legacy planning. If your advisor starts conversations with "What is important to you?" or "Where do you want to make a difference?" there is a good chance you are working with someone who can help you and who truly has your best interests in mind.

You will require someone with a strategic mind to make good decisions and provide recommendations for you and your planned giving. Philanthropists often turn to their teams of trusted experts for advice on when, how, and what to give, but you must determine whether these advisors really do have the specific expertise demanded for legacy and philanthropic planning. Your financial advisor, accountant, or lawyer may not be the best person for this task. For obvious reasons, investment advisors tend to look at what will make you the most money in the short-term rather than how to maximize the funds that will be available to the charity that matters to you now and later. Your accountant is an expert at reviewing the tax strategies that protect your current income and filing your tax returns, not planned giving. Your lawyer helps construct your will and trust(s), but they don't typically consider how they'll work with your succession and charitable plans.

"There are many ways of going forward, but only one way of standing still."

— Franklin D. Roosevelt

When I spoke with Judy shortly before her death, here's what I would have shared with her if I'd known what I know now. We hear and even use that phrase a lot, and I want to look at what it really means in this context.

If I had been able to see the future and know that Judy had just a few short months left, I would have done everything in my power to show her why she had to take immediate action.

If I had had the knowledge and experience then that I have today, I would have explained the seven most viable gifting options and how she could have used them to protect her estate, her heirs, and her legacy.

It is my hope you'll look at the next seven Big Impact Giving options and start thinking about what you could do and how soon you should take action to maximize the impact on your charity of choice and minimize your taxes.

People tend to separate their tax strategies and charitable giving decisions, but in fact, since one can, and so often does have a significant impact on the other, they need to be considered together. To get the tax receipt and avoid paying the CRA, people might make rash, last-minute charitable donations without considering whether their donation will have the maximum impact for the charity or for themselves.

As I mentioned earlier, I'm suggesting you redirect your surplus or social capital to the causes that are the most meaningful and important to you.

SEVEN BIG IMPACT GIVING TIPS:

1. GIVE CASH: Cash is a gift that is given directly to the charity and can immediately be used by the charity. In return, you receive a tax credit that you can use against your income or capital gains.

MAXIMIZE YOUR IMPACT:

If you opt to give a larger total amount and split it for donation over three to offer three to five years, it reflects your commitment to the charity.

Challenge your peers or the charity itself to use your gift as an opportunity for others to match it. The spirit of competition provides an incentive, but people may also be more inclined to give when they know that their contribution essentially doubles the original value.

⮞   THE BIG IMPACT:
    Cash allows the charity to use your gift right away!

2. GIVE SECURITIES: When you donate stocks, bonds or mutual funds the charity will — in most cases — sell them when they are received. They will have to pay some form of fee or commission for this. While not ideal, charities usually do have preferred rates with investment firms. There is however a significant benefit to you, the donor. If you donate securities that have significantly appreciated, the Canada Revenue Agency and Income Tax Act allow individuals to earn a full tax credit (based on your eligible taxable income) for the donation of securities and will not tax you on the capital gains that you would have otherwise realized through a disposition. This is a great way to release "locked up" investment capital and use it for giving while generating a useful tax credit.

MAXIMIZE YOUR IMPACT:

When donating highly appreciated securities to a charity, use the "50/50 Strategy™":

STEP ONE: Sell 50% of stock with the intent of using the funds for personal use and realize the capital gains tax on this portion

STEP TWO: Gift 50% of the stock to charity, earn your tax credit, and pay no capital gains taxes on this portion's appreciation

As a result, you unlock this "trapped" wealth, you pay capital gains taxes on the 50% you keep for yourself and you make a meaningful charitable donation that is worth more now than when you first made this investment. The charitable tax credit effectively offsets the capital gains tax owed on the entire amount.

You can take further steps to preserve your estate's assets for your heirs and ensure the charity receives a lifetime income.

STEP ONE: Use the full cash value of the sold stock plus the cash value of the tax credit earned and invest in an annuity.

STEP TWO: That annuity will produce income for you for as long as you live. You can use a portion of that income for yourself and another to invest in a life insurance policy that will be paid out to your heirs and/or your chosen cause after you're gone. The "cost" of the insurance premiums will vary for each individual and circumstance.

> ⚐ The BIG impact:
> Thanks to the sale of the securities, the investment in
> the annuity, and the purchase of the life insurance
> policy:
>
> 1. You pay *no net taxes* in the transactions
> 2. The annuity pays you an income for life
> 3. The annuity income can fund most or all the
> premiums of a life insurance policy
> 4. The value of the life insurance policy replaces the
> value of the security you sold and donated
> 5. You *make a significant gift to charity*
> 6. Your *estate is passed intact to your heirs*

3. GIVE LAND OR REAL ESTATE: If you give a piece of land
that will be held by the charity in perpetuity, the gift might be
eligible for a 100% tax credit in the donor's hands. However,
since charities are not generally experts at carrying or selling
real estate, their ability to manage this process and successfully
realize the value of the property will affect the impact of this
strategy.

MAXIMIZE YOUR IMPACT:

Making a gift of *ecologically sensitive* land for conservation
can give conservation organizations the ideal opportunity
to expand their protected land portfolio, while really
benefiting the donor.

In order to qualify, the land must be certified by the Federal
Minister of the Environment or a designated authority in
accordance with national and provincial criteria. The land,
or an eligible interest can be gifted directly to a qualified
recipient.

The value of the ecological gift is used to determine the
eligible amount of a gift for the purposes of a non–refundable

tax credit available to individuals, or a deduction from the taxable income available to corporations. As with other charitable gifts, ecological gifts may be claimed in the year of the donation and any amount not claimed in that year may be carried forward for up to five years.

To receive these tax benefits, donors must include the following documents with their federal income tax returns:

1. Certificate of Ecologically Sensitive Land, Recipient Identification, and Registered Charity Approval Pursuant to the Income Tax Act of Canada

2. A Statement of Fair Market Value of an Ecological Gift Pursuant to the Income Tax Act of Canada in support of the gifted property; and

3. An official donation receipt from the recipient charity

▶ THE BIG IMPACT:

A reduction in the taxable capital gain can be realized on the disposition of the property.

With an *ecological gift*, none of the capital gain is taxable.

Unlike other charitable gifts, there is *no limit to the total value of the ecological gifts eligible for the deduction or credit in a given year.*

4. GIVE LIFE INSURANCE: There are many ways to do this, but the first step is to *name the charity as the beneficiary of your life insurance policy.* When you die, the death benefit of the policy is paid out directly to the named beneficiary — the charity. The benefit goes directly to the charity outside of the estate of the deceased and is paid out tax free. Additionally, the estate receives a significant tax credit for the gift which can be used to reduce their tax in the final tax return.

MAXIMIZE YOUR IMPACT:

Use the Donation Multiplier™

This method of giving will help you leverage surplus wealth into a BIG IMPACT GIFT.

STEP ONE: Use your *surplus wealth* to purchase an annuity.

STEP TWO: Direct the annuity income to fully fund the premium payments for the purchase of a life insurance policy. Essentially, you are now taking a specific amount of wealth and acquiring a guaranteed source of lifetime income, which in turn will fund a tool that will provide incremental or even exponential leverage in value for some later use.

STEP THREE: Make charity the beneficiary of the policy, which will direct the payment of the death benefit to charity. This will provide your family with a much more significant legacy gift to charity, and in turn, provide a major tax credit which will ensure more of your estate stays in the hands of your heirs and not paid in taxes.

EXAMPLE:

Invest $100,000 in a life annuity. Use the roughly $5,500/year guaranteed-for-life income from that annuity to pay the annual premiums of an insurance policy (provided you clear the medicals and qualify for insurance coverage and such income rates are available at the time you implement this), with a roughly $350,000 death benefit (this is merely an example of one individual's case, the amount of coverage available and cost will vary based on age, medical clearance and insurer rates). Name your registered charity (or charities) as the beneficiary of the policy. When you die, you make an incredible legacy gift, the charity receives a $350,000 donation, and your estate in turn receives a charitable tax credit of up to $175,000. Pretty powerful stuff.

Donate a "redundant" life insurance policy

A number of people hold insurance policies that they might have put in place which are not entirely consistent with their situations today. They might have had a friend entering the insurance industry and done them a favor. They might have purchased the insurance as protection against a catastrophic event and now are financially secure and "self-insured". You might have even added excess insurance that more than covers the needs you have. Whether paid up or not, you can gift the policy you have directly to the charity during your lifetime. This gift will pay out to the charity upon the death of the insured (you), and because the charity is to be named as the beneficiary, a significant legacy gift will be paid to them. At the time the policy is *donated to the charity*, a tax credit is earned. It is valued on the recommendation of a third party valuation. There are agencies or community foundations that will help you value the gift. It will typically be determined by a number of factors focusing on the time the policy has been in effect, the funds paid into premiums and the age of the insured. When the gift is made, there might be a need to fund the cost of premiums. This can be done by the charity with other donors, or an endowment fund which could be established to create the income to fund the premiums.

> ⋗ THE BIG IMPACT:
> If they are available to you in your planned giving, powerful tools such as insurance and annuities can provide an incrementally, and even exponentially bigger impact gift. The guaranteed death benefit payout, named beneficiaries and the tax free movement of benefits outside one's estate collectively enhance the effectiveness of this giving method.

5. GIVE A BEQUEST: A bequest is any gift, for example, cash, stocks, or land that is bequeathed in a will which means the beneficiaries receive it after your death.

MAXIMIZE YOUR IMPACT:

Directing the estate/executor to gift securities or land to the charity in-kind will create significant tax credits while giving a much larger gift and will offset any capital gains taxes realized by the deemed disposition in the final tax return of the donor. The executor or trustees of the estate will not have to manage the sale or disposition of the assets, save some transactional fees, and may be able to avoid other logistical problems that might arise. While this is ideal for the donor and his/her estate, not all charities are capable of, or willing to deal with gifts in-kind, so the donor would be wise to find out ahead of time.

> ⋗ The BIG impact:
> You leave a legacy gift, earn a tax credit, and your estate is sheltered from any capital gains taxes.

6. GIVE FROM YOUR RRSP OR RRIF: As the sole surviving spouse, designate a specific charity as the beneficiary of your RRSP or RRIF.

MAXIMIZE YOUR IMPACT:

60 Second Bequest™ — Request a *"change of multiple beneficiary"* form from your plan administrator and simply add the charity, along with your heirs, as a beneficiary of your registered plan. In a very simple and convenient way, this preserves most of the inheritance for heirs, adds a gift to charity (at no cost today), and provides a tax credit for your estate to be used by your executor when filing your final tax return.

7. GIVE WITH A DONOR ADVISED FUND: A donor-advised fund (DAF) is a relatively recent income tax planning/ charitable tax credit mechanism as well as an estate planning/gifting tool that the donor opens with the help of a bank, independent financial services firm, community foundation, or a charitable foundation. The DAF acts as your own private foundation — with the DAF rather than the family taking on the asset management and administrative functions. You donate an initial amount that the DAF puts in a fund for investment, then you decide which registered Canadian charity will receive the money. You can control the timing within a given calendar year, but the foundation running the DAF might place limits or controls of how much of it will be disbursed (respecting the CRA guideline of 3.5% minimum annual disbursement rules). You are also able to make donations to your DAF at any time thereafter — including through your final estate. A DAF allows the donor to make annual decisions on charitable giving, while allowing them to receive full tax credits for contributing funds to the DAF in the year that they make the contribution and plan their estate's future.

Additionally, in most cases, DAF's can receive donations from outside parties (other family members, friends, etc.) if they wish to support your charitable directions, allowing them the same tax credit opportunity.

IMPORTANT NOTE: For Canadians to direct their DAF funds to charity, the DAF recipient must be a registered charity, in good standing, and must be Canadian, or a listed "eligible" charitable organization. This has typically been found in direction of DAF funds to US colleges or Universities.

Since most DAFs are set up using an endowment model, there is definitely a minimum and usually a maximum annual disbursement required as well. However, some organizations such as the *Benefaction Foundation* (www.benefaction.ca) might even allow donors to disburse all of their funds to charity over a very short period of time, provided certain criteria are met.

As outlined above, a DAF provides contributors with an incredible amount of flexibility. The DAF sponsoring foundation establishes your fund, administers and manages the financial assets and reporting, while the donor simply puts up the cash and decides who gets it and when.

Community foundations have some of the most robust DAF programs in the country, representing a broad range and variety of financial assets. They often have incredibly knowledgeable staff whose relationships within the community can be extremely helpful when it comes to connecting donors to charities that fit with their personal goals. Donors must understand that the foundation administers the investment funds and works closely with banks and other financial providers to manage the assets.

The Bank of Nova Scotia, TD, and Royal Bank all have their own DAF offerings as do mutual fund companies such as Investor's Group and Mackenzie Financial, but there are some restrictions, costs, and fees associated with what they'll do for you. Be sure you read the fine print and do your homework on fees, administrative costs, disbursement restrictions, and the minimum funds required.

MAXIMIZE YOUR IMPACT:

Always be aware of the fact that the cost(s) and returns have to make practical, financial sense. If the cost is disproportionately high in relation to the return on a regular basis, some reassessment may be required.

As an example, there can be investment management fees of around 1%, sometimes administration fees of up to 1%, as well as possible one-time costs and even hidden fees embedded in the investment products used. If you were to imagine a desired annual disbursement amount of as much as 5%, then any investments for the DAF portfolios would need to generate 7% to 8% in actual annual investment returns just to break even. If you add inflation to that picture, then you may need the portfolio to generate gross returns of as much as 9% to 10%. As you know, this would indicate a fair amount of investment risk over time, thus your DAF amounts could suffer significantly in falling investment markets. Costs matter and it is important that you investigate.

There are independent organizations, such as the Benefaction Foundation, which offer significant flexibility in their Donor Advised Funds plans. Benefaction, a public foundation that is registered with the Charities Directorate of the Canada Revenue Agency, provides DAFs for independent financial firms, as well as CIBC. As you would expect with an independent provider, your flexibility increases. With Benefaction, you are able to have your own investment advisor or portfolio manager continue to manage the funds. This can increase the transparency, add greater controls over the investment risk, and provide you with a little more control over management costs.

>> THE BIG IMPACT:

The DAF maximizes the returns on the funds invested to make more available for gifting. It also gives the donor the ability to allocate the gift on a timeline that realizes the necessary tax benefits, but gives the donor the time to identify a charity that truly represents their values and interests, is well-managed, and delivers tangible results.

Tax planning and charity are combined, yet the timing is separate. If retirees are dealing with new taxable and often surplus income coming from their registered plans, a DAF can assist in re-directing the surplus wealth to their favorite causes while helping to reduce the ongoing income tax concerns generated by their RRIF or pension income.

As an example, I have a number of clients with great corporate pensions and surplus wealth, who at the age of 71 will have to convert their RRSP to a RRIF and start withdrawing taxable income from the plan when they are 72. The additional surplus and taxable income moves them up into the highest tax bracket. To better manage their increased tax burden while giving charitably, they created a donor advised fund to which they can direct a portion of their surplus retirement income each year and realize a tax benefit which more than offsets the tax on the income they are receiving.

Lastly, DAFs can help ensure the philanthropic message of legacy is consistently shared with and amongst family members. The annual decision making process around which organizations and causes will benefit can give families the opportunity to talk about what they believe and which causes they want to support. Even after the person who established the fund has died, the beneficiaries (heirs) are pulled together to manage the gift(s) each year.

The DAF gives the heirs a chance to reflect on those who have passed their values and what they might have stood for, while promoting social awareness, stewardship, and a sense of social involvement.

I have provided you with a number of very specific financial strategies that can be implemented immediately. It is incredibly easy to sit around "loving mankind" but at its core, that feel-good emotion is essentially useless until it motivates you to real action that produces tangible results. It really is all about what you "do" not what you think or how you feel.

I have provided a clear set of sequential guidelines and processes to lead you through the steps required to maximize your philanthropic impact. I've provided plenty of detail over numerous pages, but I also believe it is worth summing it all up for you in the five secrets to big impact giving. As you'll see they apply as much to business and life as to philanthropy.

THE FIVE SECRETS OF BIG IMPACT GIVING

"What one does is what counts. Not what one had the intention of doing."

— Pablo Picasso

1. BE STRATEGIC:

When facing a problem that you need to address, look at why the problem exists and really work to understand what's at the root of it, how people think or feel about it, what benefits will be realized once it's resolved, and what variables can influence the outcomes.

2. BE CLEAR:

You need to clearly define and state your dreams and values to understand how they will affect who you are and the results you want to achieve. To be "ready", you must understand who and where you are right now as well as where you want to end up. When you take "aim", you are strategically establishing and focusing on your targets and at the moment you "fire", you are taking the necessary action(s) required to hit that target or apply the tactics needed to achieve that result whatever it might be.

When you are clear and strategic, you are less likely to be swayed by the passing fads and trends that affect the philanthropic sector.

3. Develop and define a repeatable process to connect ideas and strategies:

By building a consistent process you use to regularly review and identify your goals, then connecting those ideas and strategies, you will be able to more effectively solve complex problems. When you follow the same process every time, you reduce the likelihood you'll miss something or make a mistake. As importantly, the fact that you have a reliable, sequential process, system, or tool that helps you consistently realize good results can help reduce the stress and the feeling of being overwhelmed when facing a big challenge or decision.

4. Remove or minimize anything that impedes your process and progress:

En route, your progress may be affected by increased costs, unnecessary fees, bad advice, and other issues that waste your time or distract you, all of which can have a negative effect on your planned giving outcome. Learn from your missteps, avoid repeating them, and do your homework ahead of time to reduce and remove these unnecessary frictions.

5. Apply the right tactics and tools:

When you truly recognize the best solution to your biggest problems, you will more readily identify the tools you need to implement. Always understand, identify and apply the right tools and tactics to achieve the best results. A good strategic process will lead you to the right tools for the job and allow this to work for you.

Give the Gift of
Gratitude;
How Looking Back
Carries Us Forward

Gratitude, much like laughter and love, is contagious.

———————

Think of gratitude as another way of giving and really commit to giving the gift of gratitude. When you let people know how much you appreciate them, whether it's what they do for you, what they've done for others, or for simply being who they are, it lifts them up. As you express your gratitude for a terrific meal, a superb sunset, a comfortable bed, a hot shower, or any other aspect of your own life, your openness and positive attitude are sure to engage those around you and deepen your connection to them.

Gratitude is so crucial that thought leaders such as Oprah embrace it and share the benefits of expressing gratitude with others. Oprah, a woman who has so much yet has also faced so many extraordinary challenges, regularly keeps a gratitude journal where she records the five things she's grateful for each day.

Taking a moment to reflect on what warrants our gratitude demands that we free up time as well as mental and emotional space to contemplate our lives and everything around us. Reflection is the first step toward gratitude and it is vital, yet when I work with successful businessmen and women, whether they're entrepreneurs, professionals, or senior executives with high-profile firms, I've noticed they invariably focus on what's next. They are so driven that they rarely take the time to look at what they've accomplished today, let alone what they have achieved last month, last year, or five years prior.

While I do appreciate and applaud their commitment to looking ahead as they plan, push, and inspire themselves and those around them to do more and do it better, I rarely see them pause to truly reflect on their results or really celebrate their victories.

Looking back is important in business but also in life and in philanthropy. It allows us to recognize the results of our efforts and actions in order to further develop the experience, expertise, and confidence required to maintain the momentum and focus on new targets.

For all of those who openly discuss their philanthropic commitments and successes, there are likely more who do not. As much as they're passionate about the causes they support and acknowledge the results they've helped achieve, they keep it to themselves or share it only with the people that are very close to them.

Why? The reasons are as varied as the individuals themselves but undoubtedly, a number of them would say, "I don't want to toot my own horn." Or "I'm not doing it for the recognition." They may also care so profoundly about their particular cause, or it may be so deeply personal, that they keep it private.

I understand that but in my opinion, it is almost always good to be open about what matters most to us and to share our triumphs as well as our challenges.

Gratitude can help us close the circle of giving while carrying us forward. It is particularly important in the philanthropic environment because by its very nature, charitable giving is so often about expending tremendous effort to solve big problems. In most cases, the challenges remain because however many people you've helped or species you've saved, there is always so much more to be done, and in fact, the problem sometimes even worsens despite your best efforts. For example, if you are committed to providing affordable housing, that need is likely to exist in perpetuity.

For driven A-type personalities, it's difficult to express gratitude over the impact you've had if you haven't completely solved the problem and eradicated the issue. Achieving anything less than success can erode your confidence, sap your energy and even lead to feelings of hopelessness to the point you might decide to discontinue your effort or re-direct your attention to where you perceive you will get better results. This is exactly why reflection and then gratitude are so important.

In his Thanksgiving Day Proclamation in 1963, U.S. president John F. Kennedy said, "As we express our gratitude, we must never forget that the highest appreciation is not to utter words, but to live by them."

A friend of mine, Din Ladak who moved to Calgary from Kenya in the early 1970s has done exactly that. Din appreciates his life in Canada and the opportunities it has presented, while understanding firsthand the challenges faced by new immigrants as they rebuild their lives in the face of language barriers, religious and cultural differences, and harsh economic realities.

As a result, Din made a conscious decision to focus on the positive and express his gratitude by helping others in similar positions through his work in the social services sector with a focus on families and immigrants.

While serving as the Executive Director of Immigration Services Calgary, Din also started the "Immigrants of Distinction Awards" which celebrate the achievements of Calgary's immigrants every year. The public acknowledgement is important, tangible proof that hard work, innovation, and persistence will produce results that make you an integral part of your community. Recognizing their successes shows them that others appreciate what they've done while putting them front and centre where they can and do inspire others.

Din tangibly expresses his gratitude through his actions

which truly pay that gratitude forward as he continues to help families and immigrants in and around Calgary. Over the years, Din and the many immigrants he has helped inspire others to follow their lead simply by doing what they do every day, day after day.

Din's unconditional gratitude and subsequently his actions have moved others and allowed them to share a vision that is bigger and brighter than what they could ever have imagined or realized alone.

As William Arthur Ward once said, *"Feeling gratitude and not expressing it is like wrapping a present and not giving it."*

When you look at gratitude as a gift and see it through William Arthur Ward's eyes, you suddenly understand that feeling gratitude and not expressing it keeps others from understanding the impact they've had. Sharing it with everyone connects you more deeply and the act of giving increases your happiness.

Here are the *five* things that I do *daily* to share the gift of gratitude:

1. Say thank you whenever it's warranted:

Take two seconds to say the two little words that most of us don't hear often enough. Think about how you feel when someone thanks you. I don't know about you, but I will admit that every *thank you* feels good. In some situations, I go out of my way to say thank you, because I love knowing that something I said or did unexpectedly had a positive impact on another person. I can also tell you that every thank you I receive gives me the confidence and a reason to do more and do it even better.

2. Say thank you to your family and the people that matter most to you:

Let your family, friends, and anyone else that really has an effect on your life know exactly what they mean to you. Thank them for their unconditional love and share yours when you can because life is both precious and unpredictable.

3. Say thank you to those you work with or who work for you:

Even when whatever they've done is part of the job description, verbally expressing and tangibly demonstrating your gratitude for a task well done is still the right thing to do. It's also well worth telling others how much you appreciate something that was done for you by a specific individual. Again, stop and ponder the unexpected "thank you" calls, emails, notes, or texts that you've received over the years and how you felt when someone said, "I was just talking to XX and she said you'd been such a help with..." If you can give someone else the opportunity to feel that way, do it.

4. Be thankful for your accomplishments:

Recognize and acknowledge the experiences lived and the actions taken to get where you are. When you step back but look closely, you may suddenly see that what you considered minor or simply something that had to be done really does warrant more gratitude. It might feel weird or awkward to appreciate your own skills or actions, but it's what keeps you going and can help grow your confidence and subsequently, your next efforts and their results.

5. Be thankful for the challenges that lie ahead:

Embrace life's challenges rather than shying away, dreading, or resenting them and you can be sure you'll reap the rewards of that positive approach. Challenges are opportunities that help you grow, learn and expand the fullness of your life. A life without challenge is a life without impact.

Now What Will You Do?

When you give to maximize the impact, philanthropy certainly becomes a more complex process that will deliver more significant rewards to everyone involved from the donor to the recipient and beyond.

While I have encouraged you to be more thorough and thoughtful in your giving, do not allow the magnitude of the commitment to prevent you from starting today. A small progression forward is better than not taking that first step at all.

As you've seen chapter to chapter, Big Impact Giving demands that you take a logical, sequential series of steps that are designed to make sure you get it right. Over the course of your philanthropic journey, you will look into your own history and experiences to help you identify what motivates you and find the causes and organizations that really resonate with you.

Along the way, I've seen people gain a more intimate understanding of who they are and how they came to be while also forging deeply personal connections, then understanding and apply their strengths to their philanthropic endeavours to effect change.

When all is said and done, we need to be able to reflect on what we've accomplished in our lives and through our philanthropy in order to express and share our gratitude in a variety of ways. Being grateful helps maintain the momentum of our Big Impact Giving.

As you think about what you want to do and why, I want you to remember my family friends, Judy and Frank, whose wishes weren't realized because they always believed that they had more time to plan.

In a similar instance, every year I'd meet my client Dan, a widower in his eighties, to review his finances. One Friday morning, he abandoned the small talk and thought out loud about the millions of dollars he'd worked so hard to earn and the fact that neither of his well-established children, already wealthy in their own rights, needed his financial help. Dan hadn't the slightest idea of what to do with his wealth when he died. He lamented that he hadn't ever given it serious thought and now he was afraid he might lose the opportunity to make an impact.

It was such a drastic change from our usual light-hearted banter about the day's headlines and the Calgary Flames that I asked what had prompted the shift.

He explained that he had recently been diagnosed with pancreatic cancer and was expected to live just a few more months.

I nearly dropped my coffee. I was floored. It was such an emotional blow that in order to keep myself together, I dealt with Dan's announcement the only way I knew how — I suggested we meet on Monday morning to discuss his philanthropic goals, develop a plan and structure its implementation.

Three days later, we did meet and our discussion helped Dan identify the experiences that had most affected him and how they might connect him to a particular cause. I'm not sure why but I somehow thought he would figure everything out over the weekend and show up prepared to change the world with his intentions. Naturally, that was not the case, so we did what we could to move a few ideas forward. We agreed to meet again the following week, but the cancer was progressing so quickly that he had to postpone that meeting and then the one after that.

Dan died within weeks of expressing his profound desire to give back. It was such a shame, because he knew he had so much to do and so little time in which to get it done, but hadn't prepared himself for the task. In his final days he could not clearly articulate what it was he truly wanted to impact or how we should give back.

My experience with Dan and Judy and Frank reminds me of the famous Oliver Wendell Holmes quote, "Alas for those who never sing, but die with all their music in them."

If the planning process had been started earlier, Dan, Judy, Frank, and so many others would have been able to leave a lasting legacy and honor their values through BIG IMPACT GIVING.

If not now, when will you take the action required to move your philanthropy forward and realize your own BIG IMPACT GIVING?

I hope that I have inspired you and given you the tools to start the process.

Let's begin today!

Help others achieve their Big Impact Giving!

Share this book!

Retail: $14.95

Special Quantity Discounts

5 — 20 books	$13.95
21 — 50 books	$12.95
100 — 499 books	$10.95
500 + books	$9.95

To place an order, contact:

(403) 870-6775

info@BigImpactGiving.ca

www.BigImpactGiving.ca

"Buy the book"

ACKNOWLEDGEMENTS

So many people have shared so much with me over the years. Their input, wisdom, guidance and mentorship have impacted my life in so many ways. There have been so many of you, it is difficult to thank everyone, and I apologize if I did not mention. I am eternally grateful for you all.

As I reflect on all your influences, I share my thanks with my family, Sherri, Madison, Coen and my parents, Don and Maureen, first and foremost. Thank you to: Keith Thompson, James Malinchak, Scott Keffer, Dr. Danny Brassell, Kevin Clayson, Barry Spencer, Marylin Suey, Dianna Campbell-Smith, Karl Vanderleest, Kelly and Mary Aldridge, Dan Holinda, Michael Permack, W. Brett Wilson, Keith Macphail, Alvin Libin, Craig and Marc Kielburger, Malala Yousafzai, Magic Johnson, Danielle Decceco, Sam Switzer, Richard Branson, Stacey Peterson, Tony Myers, Allan Markin, Darcy Hulston, Brianne Graham, Din Ladak, Blake Mycoskie, Andre Agassi, Birgitte & Colin (in Memory of) Michie, Oprah Winfrey, Paul Alofs, Nicola Elkins, Marcella Zanella, Ainsley Grant, Nichola Lastella, Eva Friesen, Tania Loftsgard, Samantha Jones, Joann Churchill, Derek Michaels, Barbara and Brian Howes, Richard Branson, Ida June Martin.

Made in the USA
Charleston, SC
08 April 2015